In memory of Naomi

Contents

Acknowledgements

With special thanks to the students and graduates who have contributed many ideas, especially:

Sara Bishop, Gemma Charlton, Catherine Coatsworth, Pamela Cuthbertson, Christa Haddleston, Kim Hall, Millie Olcay, Suzanne Powell, Helen Smith, Dawn Taylor, Helen Waistall, Gillian Whinnam and Eleanor Whittaker.

Our thanks, too, go to the staff who have supported the development of the teaching experience on offer to our students and helped with this guide, including Allan Brownrigg, Anna Butcher, Linda Graham, Lisa Guy, Judith Kernen, Dr Pam Knights, Sue Robson, Nigel Stinton, Lindy Syson and Joan Santer.

Finally, thanks to our families, and to Jude Bowen, Amy Jarrold, and all at SAGE, for their support during the development of this book.

About the Authors

Professor Kay Sambell has 20 years' experience of teaching students about childhood at university level. She currently works at Northumbria University, where she contributes to the BA Joint Honours degree in Childhood Studies. She has published widely: both in her specialist research area (children's literature), and on her research into students' perspectives of innovative assessment. In 2002 Kay was awarded a National Teaching Fellowship by the Higher Education Funding Council for her work on assessment. She is a well-known speaker, nationally and internationally, on ways of promoting and enhancing student learning. Recently she directed a large-scale government-funded initiative aimed at improving academic literacy in Childhood Studies (the MEDAL project) and is Director of Assessment for Learning Enhancement in Northumbria University's Centre for Excellence in Assessment for Learning.

Dr Mel Gibson has, in collaboration with Kay Sambell, worked on a number of teaching and learning projects including the MEDAL project. She currently works at Northumbria University, contributing to Childhood Studies. Also a National Teaching Fellow, an award won in relation to her innovative work on bringing the 'real world' into the classroom, Mel specializes in research and teaching around young people and media. She is also a well known speaker and consultant regarding visual literacy in picture books, comics and other media. Mel has, for over 15 years, regularly advised libraries, schools and other organizations on young people, reading and visual texts. Mel has published widely in these areas for both professional and academic journals.

Sue Miller is the Lead Specialist Practitioner Family Support and Parenting Commissioner in Newcastle upon Tyne and is also an external consultant to the Department of Children, Schools and Families, supporting the delivery of family and parenting support services across the UK. She has extensive national experience in parenting education, the integration of children's services and the workforce reform issues this entails and has worked in local authorities as a teacher, senior educational psychologist, Children's Services manager and commissioner. She led on the delivery of SureStart Children's Centres in Newcastle and has had 30 years experience of working with maintained, voluntary and private providers of services for children and families. For six years she was a Senior Lecturer at Northumbria University, where she helped to develop and then went on to run the BA Joint Honours degree in Care and Education (Early Years).

Introduction

How to use this book

Here we explain what our book is for, and what it can and can't do for you. It is designed to provide students studying Childhood Studies (CS) and Early Childhood Studies (ECS) in higher education with the means to do better, to be more successful and to work towards achieving the learning outcomes of their courses with greater confidence and insight. We think you'll benefit most if you go through the chapters from start to finish, rather than just dipping into the book. Chapters 1, 2, 3, 4, and 5 are all designed to help you approach your assignments productively, by focusing on the various interrelated processes and stages of learning about childhood. Although we have, for ease of reading, teased them out into a number of different 'phases' – making the most of lectures and course materials by becoming an active learner who gets to grips with key course themes; tackling academic reading; producing a good assignment, dissertation or research project; and learning off-campus – they are, in fact, all interwoven.

These chapters are full of examples and illustrative material drawn from real courses, but you will need to use these alongside the actual material being studied on your particular course. The idea is that the examples will help you to understand your tutors' expectations, and also help you to develop strategies for tackling your course's demands. In coming to understand the key themes, issues and questions posed on your specific course, you will improve how you approach learning, and do better in your assignments.

The final chapter focuses attention on what you might want to do after your degree finishes. Thinking ahead can help you make good choices when it comes to, say, selecting topics and settings for an independent study or picking research observation visits, so reading the final chapter at the outset of your course will help you ensure that you don't close any doors for yourself when it comes to getting your dream job. The final chapter also sets out practical guidance which is designed to help take you through the process of applying for jobs and further study opportunities, and you will probably want to refer to it predominantly in your final year when you will need to make the most of your formal applications. Three years seems a long time at the start of a course, but it soon flies by, and former graduates often say they wished they had started thinking about possible opportunities and using their degree and vacation work to build up relevant experience a lot earlier than they did. This is your chance to learn from their experience, as you'll hear from these 'old hands' throughout the book, who will offer you 'insider information' about how to do well. You'll get some ideas for things you can put into action, from places to start looking for work to ways of presenting what you have learned on your course. In addition, you will hear what some previous students are doing now, what it entails, and how they got to where they wanted to be.

To summarize, then, this book should help you make the most of your time at university by helping you see the point of the degree you are studying and identifying what tutors are aiming to do in creating the courses they have. The book provides you with a set of questions to ask yourself about the degree and what you want to get out of it. These will help you 'tune in' to CS and ECS, in terms of key themes and issues, effective approaches to study, achieving your best in assessment, using your course to build up your curriculum vitae, and selling yourself well in the jobs market.

Why do you need this student guide for studying CS/ECS?

You might be wondering why we don't just outline the content of CS/ECS courses and provide you with a summary of the major points and information you need to know to pass well. One thing is that CS/ECS, like all degrees, just cannot be simplified in that way. Another reason is the rate of change in childhood policy and practice. Further, CS/ECS is quickly becoming recognized as a 'new' subject area or academic field of enquiry and a rich, complex and hugely diverse one. As a consequence, this can make it hard to get to grips with the expectations of your specific course and those who teach on it. It is, however, crucial that you suss this out if you want to do well, both on the course itself and in securing graduate employment.

Traditionally matters relating to children and childhood have been taught in universities as an aspect of several disciplines, all of which have tended to use different ways of studying children, using different methods and drawing on different ideas and principles. Some, such as education or psychology, have concentrated on the child, children or young people. Others, such as sociology or cultural studies, have concentrated on childhood as an idea or concept. Your course may actually be basically rooted in these sorts of approaches. However, the courses developing in CS/ECS have evolved their own identity and approach, which can be seen as interdisciplinary. This means that they consciously draw on the different perspectives offered by, say, sociology, social history and psychology to think about exciting new ways of theorizing childhood.

This may seem rather abstract, but to make the most of your studies, you need to be clear in your own mind of the value your course places on becoming analytical, critical and reflective, qualities also demanded in the workplace. When national policy places the child at the centre it redefines the ways in which professionals work with and relate to that theoretical child. New policy initiatives, such as the setting up of SureStart Children's Centres and the integration of Children's Services, require critical and creative thinkers who value open-mindedness and innovation.

Many courses set out quite deliberately to specifically prepare students to acquire the skills, knowledge and values of multi-professional Early Years agencies and settings. Often students are taught by tutors from a range of professions in the areas of Health, Education and Social Work. Other courses encourage students to explore different disciplinary approaches to the study of childhood, by engaging with topics as varied as children's media and books, school governance, historical archive material, parenting, social policy and representations of childhood. Students will be taught by academics including historians, literature specialists, cultural studies tutors and geographers.

We would draw your attention to the rich diversity of courses that go under the general name of CS/ECS right from the start, because, to do well, you must learn to identify the specific approach and context of your own course. Our book, therefore, sets out to encourage you to discover the key dimensions of your course thus helping you get off to a flying start. Don't assume that all courses are the same. Thinking about your course's particular outlook, aims and objectives will enable you to understand its specific expectations, allowing you to make the most of your studies, make sense of your prior and personal experiences (which all courses will value and seek to build upon) and achieve your potential. That's why we think you should try to use this book early on in your course.

We believe that thinking about your course as a whole, and even on a module-by-module level, is a fundamental aspect of success on CS/ECS programmes. In our experience students are often surprised by the particular demands of courses, especially if they expect CS/ECS to reflect more practically or vocationally oriented courses studied prior to coming to university, such as the CACHE Diploma in Childcare and Education, or if they already work with children. Consequently, some students arrive at university expecting their course to consist entirely of hands-on experience with children. Finding themselves, say, to be studying history or policy, means they feel quite lacking in confidence and even motivation, until they grasp why historical approaches to childhood or policy studies are an important aspect of their study. That courses are often rather more academic than practice-based means that far from being an easier option, CS/ECS courses demand that students read widely and work energetically on their research and academic writing skills to achieve good results.

When there is a mismatch between lecturers' understandings and students' assumptions about what it means to study childhood at university everyone has to work hard to minimize that gap. That's precisely what this book sets out to help you do, so that you can make the most of the course on which you have enrolled. It does this through helping you understand what you are expected to do, and offering strategies for undertaking the work.

The difference from vocational courses

Whatever the prevalent nature of your course is, there is no doubt that you will be expected to study different *perspectives* on childhood, explore themes of change and context, respond to questions and take part in debates. As we have already said, the various agendas surrounding childhood and children's lives are shifting: in the law, in social policy and in calls for integrated approaches to the care and education of young children in the UK. The way that CS/ECS courses engage with these agendas is what makes them distinct from those training students to be professional childcare workers such as teachers, nursery nurses or children's nurses.

This book helps you to get to grips with CS/ECS as academic courses, where you'll spend most of your time in a library or lecture room, rather than being out there applying and putting into practice skills that you need to have in a professional role. This does not mean that CS/ECS courses are irrelevant to the real lives of children, but it is important that you grasp the precise rationale for studying childhood in theory, as understanding this will stand you in good stead both during the course and later in the employment market. This is a particular focus for the chapter on working in settings and learning from placements. It is important that you use these 'real world' encounters as learning opportunities – as spaces for reflection, research and theory-building – as opposed to focusing exclusively on practical skills. The chapter is designed to help you think like a researcher, making vital connections between theory and practice.

You and learning at university – getting to grips with independent learning about childhood

This book offers insights into how best to become an effective independent learner, something that will become increasingly important as you move through your degree. Courses will change as you progress from your first to final year, with later years offering you more opportunities to work independently and with less direction from lecturers. This book will help by focusing upon the key learning processes that relate to the study of children's and young people's lives. It will outline effective, and ineffective, ways of going about study, giving you ideas for what to do and things to definitely avoid.

Throughout the book we hope to encourage you to think about the sort of learner you are and the kind of learning you enjoy, and how to develop appropriate study skills that are relevant to CS/ECS. We believe that becoming an effective self-evaluator will be key in your future professional role, indeed, it underpins the EYPS standards. To do this we will emphasize the learning *process* rather than specific content or subject matter. The book works as a 'how to' guide, by enabling you to explore the themes, issues, recurrent questions and approaches contained within your course. Use this book alongside the material you study on your course, and the specific recommended reading.

In particular, **Chapter 1** will help you understand what academic skills and qualities CS/ECS courses seek to develop in their students, and how lecturers try to facilitate that. It will introduce common key themes and issues and enable you to unpack the way that, by taking childhood as a legitimate area for study, they provide opportunities for students to 'see' that there is a wide range of different views and perspectives about what childhood is for and to 'wake up' to these differences. It will explain that the starting point for understanding another's perspective is firstly to recognize your own, and that therefore personal responses and writing can be useful ways of beginning to see, reflect on and understand childhood. It also explains that whatever the specific content or subject matter, most courses will want you, fundamentally, to *think, question, enquire* and *interrogate*. It will enable you to identify the key questions that lecturers want you to get to grips with on *your* course, help you to understand, on the most immediate level, what is meant by 'theory' and what common methods and activities tutors will use.

Chapter 2 then concentrates on reading, and gives worked examples of effective (and ineffective) approaches to reading, finding and using information about childhood. To do well at university, especially in the Social Sciences and Humanities, which tend to be writing-intensive courses, you have to be able to become fluent in the appropriate ways of talking and writing about relevant ideas and concepts in relation to your subject. The best way to do this is via talking and rehearsing ideas and practising, *before* it 'counts' in a piece of work that is going to be assessed. Talking and reading about the main themes, issues and ideas in seminars with fellow students are the first steps to writing effectively and getting good marks, so it's a mistake to see these formative activities as a waste of time.

Chapter 3 does the same for writing and presenting your ideas formally, for assessment. In our experience, those students who do well are able to see that writing at university requires them to make a transition, and they will invest a lot of thought and energy in making sure they are clear about the differences between their approaches to writing before university, and how to write on their courses. After all, another aspect of doing well is tuning in to how you are going to be expected to learn and to be assessed. This chapter will make you think about your approaches to assessment (building on earlier chapters) and allow you to hear from successful and less successful students, so that you can get the best marks possible.

Chapter 4 helps you benefit from working in settings, whether that is via placements, research observations, visits, research projects or dissertations. Successful students say this is where their learning comes alive, but it takes confidence and skill to apply your analytical and theoretical powers to complex situations. Chapter 4 helps you negotiate some of the practical, ethical and academic challenges you might encounter when learning from the real world.

Chapter 5 highlights some useful strategies for really engaging with theory/practice issues, suggesting that you try to see yourself as a researcher: someone who asks focused research questions and explores issues in depth, recognizing varying perspectives. This chapter gets you to think carefully about the sorts of research you might undertake, including your final-year dissertation, giving you pointers about useful and less effective approaches to tackling independent projects.

Finally, **Chapter 6** asks you to look ahead, during your course, to getting a job and to life after university, helping you to think and plan your studies so that you build up a body of evidence, knowledge and experience that you can capitalize on and use to help sell your skills in the workplace. It will show you how to make the most of the experiences you have to date, equipping you to build on what you already know and are interested in. This chapter will also encourage you to consider, in enough time to do something about it, whether there are other experiences or knowledge you already have or need to acquire (for example, through taking a gap year, through work experience, or through reading) that might help you to hit the ground running while on your course and, importantly, after it finishes.

1

Key Course Themes

 chapter themes

- This chapter is designed to help you to make the move to the university-level study of childhood as smoothly and swiftly as possible.

Knowing what to expect

CS/ECS courses usually attract people with a wide range of prior experiences, and so students are likely to have an equally wide spectrum of feelings about studying childhood at degree level. Some may lack confidence because it seems that many of their peers have previously taken child-focused courses, while they have not. Others may initially feel that they're being asked to cover old ground and that they know the subject well already.

This chapter shows that no matter what you have done before coming to university, *everyone* has something new to learn, adjustments to make and study skills to develop. No matter how much, or how little, prior experience of studying childhood or working with children you have, you will usually need to adjust your thinking, and your approaches, to study so that you can contribute and draw from the new learning opportunities university study affords. Indeed, you may well hear lecturers say that they are still learning about childhood themselves, because the sort of learning you do at university is never 'done' – there are always new insights to be gained and connections to be made.

It's worth remembering, too, that *everyone* has valuable experiences to offer. We hope by the end of this chapter you will see how much you have to gain from developing good working relationships with your fellow students, as well as your lecturers.

How can you tell what your course's approach is?

Where is it located?

The first thing to do is to identify where your course is taught within the structure of academic disciplines in your university. Broadly speaking, CS/ECS is usually taught under the umbrella of Social Sciences and Humanities, but you can learn a lot by getting a closer focus on it than this.

One way of sorting this out in your own mind is by looking at which School, Department or Faculty your course sits in. For example, is it in Education, Health, Cultural Studies or Social Studies? Is it offered in just one department, or a few? Getting answers to all these questions can tell you a lot about the sort of emphasis it is likely to have.

Who teaches on the course and what are their particular research interests?

What a lecturer's discipline and research interests are is not always apparent to a student, but it is important because each discipline has its own academic outlooks and perspectives, and this has an impact on what is taught and so on what you need to know to do well. So, for instance, an individual who teaches you may view themselves as primarily a historian, an anthropologist, a psychologist and so on and that will influence the course. On the other hand, your course may be taught mainly by professionals who are trained to work with children and families (such as qualified teachers, health visitors, playworkers, social workers) and will base their teaching on those professional perspectives. Finally, the course might quite consciously set out to offer you a mix of professional and academic perspectives on the child. We will help you identify your lecturers' perspectives by looking carefully at the words they use to describe the study of childhood and finding out what terms they find problematic or even offensive. You can start, though, by looking up their publications, either through an online bookshop, or, even more usefully, by looking at the university website, which should offer both biographies and bibliographies of the staff teaching on your course. What they write and what their professional background is should help you to find out whether their

CS/ECS teaching is the main aspect of their job, or if they teach on other courses too.

What approach does your course take as a whole?

Many of the people who work on CS/ECS courses would class their work as interdisciplinary. However, they won't all mean the same thing by 'interdisciplinarity'. Sometimes they will mean you get to study childhood from different academic disciplinary perspectives, sometimes they will try to meld this into a holistic approach. Some courses concentrate on the many diverse ways childhood is viewed with regard to time, place, age, ethnicity and other variables. CS/ECS can also be informed by a critique of the ways in which children's lives are governed, regulated and dominated by adults. Courses may also be underpinned by an emphasis on children as participants in society and decision-makers – and consequently will have a child-centred approach or children's rights as a dominant theme. Asking yourself, 'where does my lecturer stand in relation to this?' or, 'do all my lecturers agree, or do they have quite different viewpoints?' will help you to sort this out. In asking these questions you will start to develop a reflective approach to your course.

You and the course themes

Generally speaking, the new student of childhood must learn to take a *thematic* approach to study. Childhood is the theme at the core of your study, but there are lots of different ways of approaching that theme. Students on CS/ECS courses are encouraged to engage simultaneously with a range of interlinked disciplinary perspectives, which means they might be expected to draw on recent research and theories including sociology, psychology, cultural studies, social history, philosophy, social policy and children's rights. This also means that students have to 'know their way around' a whole host of disciplines and the different ways they talk about childhood, and be able to use the different patterns and ways of constructing and talking about the knowledge that these contain. As you read across a number of disciplines you will discover an extensive lexicon of terminology, approaches and conventions, in what can be described as a 'joined up' approach to study.

In very practical terms, the thematic approach means you will have to learn to navigate round a large number of areas of the library, as texts on childhood will appear in all of them, rather than being located together. Chapter 2, 'Reading into Writing', guides you through the tricky process of managing the various languages used by different academic cultures, which you will need to learn to use in your writing if you wish to do well.

Problematizing childhood

Making the move to studying childhood at university, however, basically involves seeing childhood in new and increasingly complicated ways. Most courses will encourage you to identify and take stock of what you already know about children and childhood, whether that is theoretical knowledge, the practical work of bringing up children, professional practice, or your own experience of being a child. Your lecturers, though, are likely to move you gradually away from personal to more theorized views of children and their lives, encouraging you to see childhood as a complex, problematic concept, rather than as a straightforward, natural phase that we all go through. This chapter highlights some of the ways they might encourage you to see childhood afresh, waking up to 'taken-for-granted' notions about children and childhood.

In short, your lecturers are looking for far more than commonsense ideas, or a set of facts about children's development: they eventually want you to be able to analyse children's lives and environments; the products and policies that are made for them; their experiences and the views of professionals who work with and for them. In a nutshell, they will want you to be able to analyse ideas and meanings associated with 'the child' and 'childhood' and to see that talking about childhood is actually a very demanding thing to do. They will hope that during your time at university you will get deeply involved in exploring, discussing and debating a range of varying ideas and perspectives on the meanings of childhood.

key point

The words lecturers might use to describe this process include:

As an idea childhood is	Discussing it is
• Contested	• Intricate
• Problematical	• Complicated
• Complex	• Involved
• Debatable	• Discursive
• Challenging	• About perceiving key questions, rather than seeking answers or final solutions to problems

The implications: there's no 'correct' answer

From your viewpoint as a student, it's crucially important that you grasp this, because it means there is rarely a single correct answer to the assignments that are set. Put bluntly, it means that no one can tell you what you should put in an assignment. Studying childhood at university, therefore, is not a case of simply knowing and remembering facts, but being able to show that you genuinely understand complexity, can question everything and shift between diverse viewpoints.

However, although there may be no right or wrong answers, from an examiner's point of view, there are certainly better and worse ways of producing good assignments about childhood. The rest of this chapter is geared to helping you get off to a flying start, by assisting you in using the teaching sessions, your experiences, your peers, your lecturers and all the activities offered on your course productively.

What will the teaching of childhood be like?

When people first come to university they typically anticipate more structure. They expect to sit in huge, tiered lecture halls, simply writing down whatever pearls of wisdom the lecturer utters. Studying CS/ECS is rarely like that. Besides, this is a very passive learning strategy which won't help much. Instead, you will be expected to play a highly active role within and beyond the classroom. Whilst you may find you have relatively little scheduled class time, compared to students on other degrees, you will be expected to undertake a lot of independent or directed study. Becoming an active learner is the key to success.

key point

What is an active learner?

Active learning is an approach or a learning strategy. It means becoming:

- **Personally involved** – for example, by trying to understand a range of viewpoints, recognizing debates, doing things which help you to make sense of your learning about childhood, discussing ideas, linking information/ concepts and looking for patterns of ideas, linking your learning to what you know.
- **Critical and analytical** – for example, by not taking things at face value, always asking 'why?', examining beliefs about childhood from many angles, comparing the same issue from different theorists' points of view, being attuned to hidden agendas, weighing up the arguments for and against something, looking for contradictions.

- **Creative** – for example, by applying your imagination, searching for connections and patterns, asking questions, being curious, thinking laterally, weighing up how others see things, thinking critically and analytically.
- **Reflective** – for example, by analysing and evaluating your own experience and performance, being able to draw lessons from it.
- **Self-regulating** – for example, by effectively managing your own time, priorities and resources, evaluating your work and monitoring your own learning.

All these aspects interrelate, and will, importantly, help you develop personally to meet the challenges of graduate employment.

As a result, then, expect to change. Even if you already have lots of practical experience, you should soon begin to see things very differently as an active learner, questioning your practices and beliefs about children and childhood as you think more deeply about the issues and the possible implications of different theories or ideas.

You are likely to find a mixture of teaching methods used in scheduled class time. These are outlined in Table 1.1, together with some tips for how (and how not) to approach each one.

Table 1.1   Common teaching methods and how to approach them

Type of session	Description	Do	Don't
Lectures	Usually for large numbers of students. Will cover core ideas that everyone needs to get their heads round. May be interactive – breaking up for small-group discussion, question-and-answer sessions or debates. N.B. 'Lectures' are often used as a general term for any teaching session.	Prepare in advance. If the lecturer has set reading, get hold of it and make notes on anything you don't understand. Pick up clues about the key aims of the session. Make notes on the main points, issues, controversies and ideas and afterwards discuss with other students over coffee. Date and sort these afterwards into files for each module. Join in with discussion activities. If there is a Powerpoint on the E-Learning portal, download it before the lecture and take it along. You can then simply add your own notes to it.	Simply copy down whatever the lecturer says or puts on overheads. Just turn up and hope that'll be enough.

Table 1.1 (Continued)

Seminars	Tend to ask you to work on pre-prepared material. Might ask you to present your ideas, sometimes in groups.	Do your homework and go to the session prepared, even if it's not 'marked' – joining in will really help you develop your understanding before it 'counts' in assessed work. Make notes on the feedback you get, from peers as well as tutors.	Let yourself and your fellow students down by being ill prepared and not contributing to discussions.
Tutorials	Tend to be your chance to set the agenda and talk about your problems, gain feedback on your ideas when preparing an assignment or discuss your progress and devise action plans.	Prepare notes beforehand of things you want feedback on (e.g. an essay plan, uncertainties you have about core concepts or reading for a module). List questions you want to ask about to help you better understand the topic (e.g. getting clarification on a theory).	Ask procedural questions that can be answered elsewhere (e.g. word limits, deadline dates, where to hand in assignments – your course administrator or handbooks can tell you). Expect your lecturer to cover material from a lecture that you missed.
Directed study	This is like 'homework', which you do out of class contact time, although it's rarely taken in or marked. Expect to spend a lot of time on this and on more general reading round (usually called 'independent study'), as it helps you make sense of sessions and is crucial to producing good assignments.	Make sure you do it, as it will help you make the most of teaching sessions. Talk about it with other students. (See Chapter 2, 'Reading Into Writing', for guidance.)	Put it off or rely solely on formal contact time if you want to do well in your assignments.

These methods may seem less directive than those you experienced at school and college – and it can be hard not having anyone nagging you to turn up, but it's hugely important to realize that;

- the lectures are important in enabling you to perform well
- tutors expect you to do much more than simply turn up to sessions.

We'll now turn to why this is the case, and how you can make the most of what is on offer.

Why go to lectures?

On any course students need to become alert to the ways in which things are done in their particular subject area. In CS/ECS courses you will need to get yourself tuned in to the following ways of knowing about childhood:

- Knowing yourself
- Knowing your lecturer
- Knowing the subject/content.

In the rest of this chapter we'll explain what we mean, and how you can use lectures to best effect to help you build up these ways of knowing.

Knowing yourself: personal views of childhood

It's useful to think of learning to study childhood at university as a sort of journey. Achieving the complexity, subtlety and questioning approach to CS/ECS that we outlined at the beginning of this chapter usually means starting initially with what we know and experience at an individual, personal level. Most CS/ECS courses will, therefore, begin the course, and probably most modules, by first identifying and then questioning or challenging your own relevant personal experience in particular contexts. The following examples are designed to give you a flavour of the sorts of activities lecturers may use to help you take this initial step on the road to theorizing childhood.

Identifying personal views of the child

You will probably undertake introductory tasks and class activities that help you to identify your own opinions and views of the child-related topics lecturers are teaching. Firstly, lecturers will usually want to show you that when we look at a child we may think that we all see the same thing. We don't. What we see depends on what we bring to the situation – our personal 'baggage'.

We all have values and beliefs about what is proper, right and good for children, values that will usually relate to our own experiences. Often we will not have really thought about them, assuming instead that they are 'just the way things are'. Lecturers will typically want you to start to see these views and opinions as 'loaded' and problematic. For this reason, it's important when studying childhood to identify and know about your own views.

to think about

Identifying your personal views and values by talking with fellow students

Here, for example, is a student talking about the age at which, in her opinion, children should start school:

> We send children to school properly at five. They need to learn to read and write, and the earlier they start the better, because otherwise they'll fall behind. And no one can get by these days without being able to read and write properly.

This student was taken aback to find that another student in her discussion group was outraged at the prospect of sending children into formal education so young:

> In Norway we don't force children to read and write until they're ready. They need to play and enjoy life and find out who they are and how to get along with other people first. They learn to read and write when they're about seven.

Neither student really noticed what they took for granted about children's needs, until they discussed it. This is why your peers are so important: you can all help each other begin to register the complexity of studying childhood.

Getting involved in class discussions about people's views and beliefs helps us to see how variable these are. You are on the right lines if you start to question what you previously 'knew' – or failed even to register – beforehand. Students often say studying childhood is like suddenly waking up, and hence is very different from previous study.

It makes you think a lot more, think in different ways. There are things you accept before you come here that you don't happen to think about, unless you study this course. Things occur to me now, that I wouldn't have thought about before – in everyday life. Like, you're watching children in society, all the time. How they're treated.

case study

Thinking about the words we use

You might get asked to identify your personal opinions, values and attitudes by noting your personal feelings and reactions to, say, a video clip of children, or some images.

In this example, for instance, a lecturer shows her class a video of a child with her mother, shopping in a supermarket. The child can be seen running up and down the aisles of busy shoppers, gathering armfuls of goods from the shelves and pushing the trolley in all directions.

Students then write down what they see, and then compare and contrast their notes. Usually, their views will vary. Some will see the girl as 'naughty' and feel sorry for the mother, who they will view as not being able to control her daughter, or as being subject to other shoppers' views of her 'poor' parenting skills.

A naughty little girl is banging her trolley into other people's trolleys. The poor mother is embarrassed, because everyone is staring, especially when the little girl has a tantrum.

The girl is behaving like she's spoiled: the mum should stop her. She's being a real nuisance.

Others' sympathies will lie with the child.

I remember the boredom of going shopping as a child – at least this little girl is managing to liven things up! She's just having fun!

The point is that different students will bring different things to analyse exactly the same incident. The difference lies in their *values, attitudes and assumptions* about what makes a 'good' mother, about how children should behave, about what children are like and how they should be treated.

Note how the words they use reveal this: '*poor* mother'; '*naughty* girl', '*just* having fun'. These words show their views of the child are far from neutral. It is, therefore, invariably a useful exercise to think carefully and critically about the words people use to describe children and childhood.

Tuning in to these words helps you to see where people might be coming from when they talk, and later write, about CS/ECS topics.

When you come to write your assignments, lecturers will expect you to 'define your terms' – to show that you know that there are many different ways of viewing a phenomenon, and can spell out clearly the ways in which your essay uses a word or term. We will talk more about this in later chapters, but it's important that you realize that many of the informal in-class exercises that will be set are to encourage you to practise thinking about the ways in which words and images used to discuss and describe children and childhood are deeply loaded with significance.

Making the familiar strange

Lecturers will often get you to jot down notes about your prior knowledge of the child and childhood. You might be asked, for instance, to write down, as quickly as possible and in no particular order, all the words that spring to mind in response to the question, 'What is a child?'

 case study

'What is a child?'

Here's what some students wrote:

Innocent	Cute	Enthusiastic
Curious	Friendly	Loveable
Playful	Happiness	Dependent
Vulnerable	Carefree	Small
	Fun	Always learning

The lecturers then prompted students to think about how these words, on the whole, combined to create a hugely idealized image of the child. To show how 'loaded' the words are, they asked students to think about the implications for real children.

In fact, the first set of words mostly construct the child as perpetually happy, leaving no space for children to be sad (what if their pet has just died?); bored (what if they have to sit through a dull set of wedding speeches?); or knowing (what if they've been involved in bullying at school?). Among other things, this can exert a potentially huge pressure upon real children.

(Continued)

(Continued)

Students realized the extent to which the words and ideas that spring to mind to describe the notional child are often very biased, and, when taken altogether in this sort of exercise, reveal common generalizations about children. The artificiality of the exercise, which doesn't ask students to relate to 'real' children, heightens this, but it usefully shows how far adults have *abstract ideas about the meanings of childhood* that result in stereotypes about children. Often, as in this case, these ideas reflect dominant beliefs: commonly held values, attitudes and assumptions. This exercise, then, moves students' knowing from the tacit (taken for granted) to the explicit, making them question, once more, what they already think they know.

Life maps and timelines

A personal timeline   Another common exercise to get you thinking about your personal views of childhood is to get you to draw a line like the one below, asking you to mark key milestones on the line, as you moved from childhood to adulthood.

Myself as Child --Myself as Adult

Don't enter any information you would rather not share in these sorts of exercises: lecturers are not asking you to dig up unhappy memories. People usually put things like 'started school', 'moved house', 'best friend moved', 'passed driving test', 'pet died', 'parents divorced', 'rented own flat' and so on.

When these are compared and contrasted you'll probably notice some broad similarities in childhood experience (especially if people have fairly similar backgrounds and cultures), but large discrepancies on a personal level. This helps you see the point that childhood is a relative, variable entity, dependent on an individual's personal experience. Put simply, no two childhoods are actually the same.

Timelines from childhood to adulthood   This is a similar exercise, but more general, noting the milestones many children can be expected to pass and dividing the timeline up into stages. Students put things like 'weaned', 'started walking', 'learned to read', 'went to school', 'take SATs', 'move from primary to high school', 'first date', 'able to drink alcohol', 'learned to drive', 'allowed to have sex', 'start periods', 'leave school', 'can get married', 'allowed to vote', 'first job', 'go to college' and so on.

Discussion usually focuses on a wide range of different conceptual categories that can be used to define childhood. These might include:

- Biological and developmental definitions – for example, weaned, started walking, puberty, physiological changes. These often lead to stage definitions – babyhood, toddler, middle childhood, adolescence, young adulthood.
- Institutional/educational definitions – for example, pre-school, nursery-aged child, primary-school pupil, high-school pupil, school-leaver, college student.
- Age definitions – 0–3, under 5s, 7–11, pre-teens, teenagers, young adults.
- Legal definitions – age at which allowed to have sex, drink, smoke, drive, etc.
- Gender definitions – girlhood might be qualitatively different to boyhood.

Reflecting on personal experience usually prompts debate about the extent to which 'real' children actually conform to these definitions and norms. In particular issues around:

- Social values, attitudes and beliefs about children (especially their status, how far they are seen as dependent and incompetent, or capable and independent).
- Personal beliefs about how far children 'need' to conform to these milestones.
- What happens to children who don't, or cannot, conform (e.g. how disabled children are seen when they don't meet developmental 'norms').

You need to learn to tune into the nature of these debates in each module, because they will furnish you with essential information about your tutor – what they see as important, what issues they want you to understand and be able to discuss and so on.

Knowing your lecturer and knowing the subject/content

These two things are often intertwined, as we'll show you. Lecturers will encourage you to question and interrogate taken-for-granted meanings around childhood through exploring personal values, as we have seen above. Don't assume, though, that because lecturers ask for your personal experience, they want you to express unconsidered opinions in your assignments. What they want you to do is to learn to *theorize* what you say. To do well in their assignments you must get to know their expectations about theorizing material. In this sense, knowing your lecturer is not about knowing them as a person or buttering them up so they'll give you better marks, but about making sure you fully understand their expectations about the subject, the content and how it is discussed.

This is more complicated than it sounds because every lecturer will have their own disciplinary and/or professional approach to talking academically about childhood and children. You need to tune yourself in to the ways in which they theorize the subject area. These can vary dramatically from tutor to tutor and from course to course, so it's important for you to remain sensitive to the concepts, terminology and issues they wish you to discuss in the assignments they set. You will need to use these to show that you have moved beyond personal opinions when you come to tackle your assignments, because you will be marked down if you offer untheorized opinions.

But how do you know what each lecturer wants?

Going to lectures is the key to finding out each lecturer's theoretical approach to the subject: what counts as theory, for them, and how they define the nature of the subject or field of enquiry. You can fathom this out by thinking about the following things.

Identifying your lecturers' key course themes and issues   The first step is to make sure you grasp the *issues* each lecturer wants their students to explore. Your assignment should relate to these. Specific issues will reflect the focus of the subject area of the degree, or even lecturers' individual research interests, hence these can vary immensely. Certain ones will crop up in different guises, though, as common course themes, threads and key issues.

 to think about

Some examples of common course themes might be:

- power, control and decision-making on behalf of children
- status
- children's perspectives and viewpoints
- motivation
- ownership
- families
- inclusion and equal opportunities
- play
- citizenship and participation
- parenting

- gender
- learning (formal, informal and unintended, e.g. the hidden curriculum)
- growth and development
- autonomy
- children's rights and agency
- policy and practice
- leadership and management
- adults' roles (professional perspectives, parents' views, censorship)
- choice
- success and failure.

James and James (2008) and Nutbrown (2005) offer useful further suggestions and starting points.

Identifying your lecturers' theoretical stance to the subject area they teach   The reading list reveals any tutor's key concepts, viewpoints and approaches to studying childhood – and will equip you with the main 'tools' your tutors want you to use. We look at this in detail in the next chapter. The easiest way to begin, though, is to pay careful attention to what goes on in formal sessions. Here your lecturers will tend to introduce you to the perspectives and theories that interest them in more formal ways.

They'll tend to do this by presenting *conflicting perspectives*. On CS/ECS courses it's important to identify and talk about diverse perspectives, because this is the first stage of beginning to 'get into' any area being studied. In lectures, therefore, look out for the *key questions* each lecturer highlights or poses for you to discuss. This is where tutors will really reveal the issues they want you to explore, and the concepts and terminology they want you to use. Time spent after sessions thinking carefully and making notes on the nature of these questions and debates – the big ideas – will be time well spent and improves your chances of doing well in assignments.

We'll now move on to think about how your lecturers might do this.

Introducing you to starkly different or contrasting views of the child

Many courses will introduce students to the different models, concepts or images of the child that can best be seen by comparing the differences between time, place, culture and so on. Historical approaches help us see how the child was/is seen as a special category of people, increasingly regarded as essentially different from adults, and viewed in relation to other social categories, such as gender (is girlhood different from boyhood?), class (is an unemployed or working-class childhood different from a middle- or upper-class childhood?), ethnicity (is childhood different according to ethnic group?). It also helps us see how far, and in what ways, childhood is viewed as being different from (or similar to) adulthood in various contexts.

to think about

Historical constructions of the child

You may be asked to think about current ideas about childhood by reflecting on historical views of the child. This is because it is argued that social and historical factors have an important bearing on the experience of being a child. We can consider what meanings adults have associated with childhood as a state of being and begin to analyse the ways in which attitudes towards children have changed and developed by looking at representations of childhood across time.

For example, we can see that the state of being a child shifts if we think about differences in how long, say, childhood lasts. In Western countries nowadays we might expect children to start to play a formal economic role at the age of 15 or so, while in the past children as young as 6 went out to work.

Furthermore, at different times childhood could be seen, for example,

- as a time of Romantic innocence, during which children should learn naturally, protected from the polluting influences of adult institutions and ideas.
- as innately evil, with Evangelical adults needing to be 'cruel to be kind' to ensure that children follow the path to righteousness and proper moral conduct.
- as a time in which children are like blank slates ('Tabula Rasa') waiting for adults to give them knowledge and make them learn.
- as under threat, with particular cases, such as Baby P or the Victoria Climbie inquiry, prompting massive public concern and policy developments around children's well-being and safeguarding.

Always think carefully about the questions your lecturer is highlighting if they present you with starkly contrasting perspectives. Are they highlighting questions relating to cultural determinants (e.g. gender, class)? Or are they highlighting questions relating to children's agency (children's voices, power, status)? Are they highlighting questions of policy, professional practice and change (what are the challenges of implementing the

ECM agenda)? Or are they focusing on questions surrounding the representation of childhood (tensions between Romantic conceptions of the
child as innocent and the child as knowing, debates about portrayals of
the child in poetry, comics or other media)?

Recognizing the diversity of Childhood/Early Childhood Studies as a subject area

Activities and reading that help students think about the variable ways in
which childhood can be interpreted are important to CS/ECS as an emergent
field. Lecturers will often set such activities because they help students to
perceive key questions about the meanings of childhood. Once more, seeing
different points of view can help learners recognize, sharply and often with a
shock or a jolt, how they think and feel about the 'reality' of childhood today.
This makes us ask questions such as:

- What makes someone seem childish or childlike?
- What behaviour is regarded as 'appropriate' for children?
- What is a child's nature really like? (Are children innately evil or inherently good?)
- Who 'owns' childhood and who governs it? How should children be treated?
- What is good for children?

All this draws attention to the crucial importance of *adults'* ideas about the
meanings of childhood, which may not be what you expect to be studying. In
fact, many of the questions on CS/ECS courses will revolve around how
adults see children: the meanings they ascribe to them and the ways in which
they treat them.

It's worth emphasizing, that, as a consequence, the academic study of
childhood often focuses on *representations,* stories and concepts – ideas –
about the child (in line with disciplines such as sociology, English and cultural studies), as well as focusing (as with disciplines such as education or
psychology) on the child or children *per se.* You are looking for the hidden
meanings, if you like, whether the focus of study is representational art about
children, or products for children (paintings, fiction, magazines), or 'real-life'
interview data (professionals, parents or children talking about childhood).

Perspectives on childhood

Most courses nowadays will have a module that introduces varying views of
the child, and highlights diverse perspectives on the meanings associated

with childhood. Such modules aim to get you thinking about the hugely different ways in which childhood as an idea can be seen.

The words lecturers will probably use to highlight this common theme include:

perspectives	paradigms
views	conceptions
images	ideologies
models	ideas
theories	notions
versions	discourses
constructions	perceptions
concepts	interpretations ... of childhood.

Identifying the key issues within a module

Getting to know your lecturer also means tuning in to how far your lecturer is interested in studying children as 'real' embodied individuals, perhaps in particular professional contexts or settings, or how far they expect you to explore more general ideas about concepts of childhood in a more abstract sense. Again, thinking about the focus of their lectures and the key debates or questions they expect you to be able (eventually) to discuss and theorize in a scholarly, academic manner in your assignment will give you a good idea. They will usually start, however, by getting you to simply see that there is a debate to be had.

Often they will refer to key debates, or even set up debates for you to hold among yourselves in class. Recognizing these is the key to success.

 case study

Identifying the key issues – Child Development

A lecturer teaching Child Development was keen to introduce her students to 'great' researchers: people like Piaget, who had conducted experimental research, observing children and drawing up theoretical viewpoints. She was concerned, however, that because a lot of her students would feel that they 'already knew' about these theories from previous courses, they would tend to simply regurgitate the researchers' accounts of the 'ages and stages' in the assignment they produced. This was not at all what she wanted – instead she expected her students to *stand back and question* psychologists' interpretations of the factors that impact on children's development. This, for her, was theory.

To highlight this she based her lectures on key themes, such as the extent to which various theorists saw the role and relative importance of genetic or environmental factors in children's development. In sessions she encouraged students to compare and contrast different theorists' views of the ways in which children are understood to develop, change, grow and make sense of the world. The questions she raised in sessions surrounded:

- How do different researchers and theorists (Locke, Skinner, Bandura, Vygotsky, Freud, Piaget) believe that children learn?
- How does each explain children's emotional, social and intellectual growth?

The essay title she set was 'Piaget was a psychologist who explored factors that impact on children's development. Discuss his findings in the light of relevant literature'. Poor essays were those in which students simply gathered and copied down information about Piaget's stages. Essays that received good marks discussed Piaget's ideas by recognizing them as part of a *debate* about the relative importance of nature and nurture.

 case study

Identifying the key issues – Children's Rights

A lecturer teaching Childhood and Human Rights wanted to encourage students to think about the complexities involved in coming to decisions which could be deemed to be 'in the best interests of the child'. After outlining the series of markers laid down by the UN Convention, her sessions focused on how children are constructed in the minds of adults and the relationship between this and the implications for social policy and practice in the care, education and health of children within both the family and the wider community.

In sessions she got students to discuss and debate issues of power: who holds it, how is it accessed, what is the commitment to power sharing? One

(Continued)

(Continued)

debate, for example, focused on the 'Gillick Case', which students were asked to read about before the session. The lecturer asked one group to make the case that girls under the age of 16 should have access to contraception without their parents' knowledge. She asked the other group to put the view that this would encourage promiscuity and the promotion of under-age sex to people who might not be emotionally ready.

In this way the lecturer encouraged students to think about who they thought should decide and why, as a first step to identifying the issue and perceiving the debate, which hinges essentially upon the different views of the child. She was not looking, ultimately, for a gut-response or an opinion, but for a reasoned response, acknowledging different points of view. Other sessions were used to model similar debates, by presenting different perspectives on whether a disabled child's 'best interests' would be served by attending a special or a mainstream school, and on whether conjoined twins should be separated, if the operation risked the result of only one twin's survival.

The lecturer hoped that by setting up in-class debates students would be clear about why she would give very low marks to an assignment that simply regurgitated the principles of the UN Convention, and why she expected essays to discuss and debate the complexities and problems involved in decision-making on children's behalf. The next two chapters will explain the ways in which she hoped students would move beyond the broad, rather emotive debates initiated in her teaching sessions, into theorizing different perspectives via reading, but for now it's important to recognize that the sessions acted as important signals to cue-sensitive students about the nature of the issues this lecturer hoped to raise.

Exploring policy issues

As we said earlier, CS/ECS courses are likely to require you to study *adults'* views and assumptions on childhood. Adults' beliefs, approaches and the views of policy-makers are common themes in CS/ECS, because children's worlds and environments are heavily shaped, and constrained, by what adults want, or the ways in which adults believe children and young people should be treated.

Child-centred consultation (seeking children's views and seeing them as people *now* rather than as just miniature adults-in-the-making) is another issue which will emerge in different areas within your course. The questions here might be:

- How can you, in policy terms, balance the tensions between seeking to protect children while including them in decision-making?
- Who decides what is in a child's best interest, when parents, professionals and the child cannot agree?

These two themes are academically significant, as they demand that the student engages deeply with key ideas and beliefs about childhood. They are also significant professionally in relation to policy developments.

Every Child Matters: New contexts, new professionals, new challenges

It's a very exciting, interesting and challenging time for CS/ECS in the UK, as in recent years, public attention and national policy have focused on children and childhood at a range of levels and across a number of professions. As a consequence of this focus there is, and will continue to be, an impact:

- on the sorts of jobs that are available
- on the kinds of professionals who are needed
- on the sorts of courses universities make available.

'Every Child Matters: change for children' is a core policy approach to the well-being of children from birth to the age of 19. The aim is that every child, whatever their background or circumstances, has the support they need to meet the Every Child Matters (ECM) outcomes, which are to:

- be healthy
- stay safe
- enjoy and achieve
- make a positive contribution
- achieve economic well-being.

This means that organizations providing services to children are being asked to work together in new ways, sharing information. The ECM agenda implies deep-seated structural and cultural change, so issues relating to the restructuring of the children's workforce, principles of leadership and management, health and welfare, and the implementation of integrated and multi-agency working will be a key focus of many courses.

An integral part of ECM is the Common Core Framework of Skills and Knowledge for the Children's Workforce. This aims to reflect a set of common values and define the knowledge and basic skills needed by those working with children and families. The Common Core sets out six areas of expertise which everyone working with children should have. They include:

- effective communication and engagement
- child and young person development
- safeguarding and promoting the welfare of the child
- supporting transitions
- multi-agency working
- sharing information.

These areas will appear as central and recurrent themes on your course and you are likely to be given lots of opportunities to reflect deeply on them and debate how they might be viewed and interpreted. It's important to engage actively and questioningly, however, rather than see your learning as a straightforward set of knowledge that you will be given or you will acquire. The following chapters will help you develop effective strategies to accomplish this.

Further, ECS is a particularly rapid growth area. New legislation is affecting practitioners on a daily basis, and the sheer pace of change means they may well be struggling to keep abreast of developments, whilst you will have a chance to study and consider them in detail. The Foundation Stage of Education (3–5) now affords the early years of education a distinct identity and importance. The Effective Provision of Pre-School Education (EPPE) project, which demonstrated the effects of high-quality provision on children's development, has contributed to the belief that a graduate-led workforce will improve children's outcomes. As integrated and holistic services are being developed, and the profile of childcare is significantly raised, early years' practitioners' roles and responsibilities are changing apace as are the potential career pathways for those interested in working with and for children. For instance, Early Years Professional Status (EYPS) offers the potential to become a change agent who will help to raise the quality of provision. All these changes require dedicated, creative, imaginative and reflective thinkers, who can understand, interpret and respond sensitively to complex situations.

It's worth remembering, then, that you, as a current student, will be one of the professionals meeting these challenges. As we will discuss in the final chapter, doing any degree enables you to develop a range of valuable graduate skills, but as ECS/CS students you have the chance to work and reflect on issues specifically relating to relevant policy, child development, the challenges of partnership working, professional and leadership roles. This will help you work towards becoming a critical practitioner who can make a difference in settings, but you need to be active, within and beyond the university classroom, rather than sitting back and passively waiting for learning to happen. Above all, you must make sure you become familiar with your course's aims so that you make the most of what's on offer.

Learning to ask yourself questions about why things are as they are, why change is challenging, why people hold certain values, or how people construct and reveal views of children's needs is essential to studying CS/ECS. It means you're being analytical and critical. If you get into the habit of using sessions to tap in to the relevant issues, identifying the 'big questions' and rehearsing your responses to different ways of addressing them, you should be well placed to successfully tackle the reading and assignments. This is because you will start to see what *you* need to know and be able to do on each module, which will enable you to take the next fruitful steps.

Look for issues not answers: 'it depends'

In short, your course is likely not to give you 'answers' but to *raise issues*. CS/ECS is, increasingly, all about problematizing what can be made to sound extremely easy: doing the right thing by our children, whether as carers, policy-makers, educators or parents. You will no doubt study provision, policy and legislation on your course, but you must learn to adopt a critical, academic eye when you look at these, too. Again and again, you should realize that whatever is done on behalf of children is far from simple: it all depends on how you see it.

It's therefore very important to perceive the steps that can help you to become critical and analytical when studying children and childhood. 'Critical' in this context does not mean you have to disagree with everything, it means weighing up and thinking questioningly about other people's ideas, looking for the meanings beneath the surface, contrasting different interpretations and people's values, attitudes, principles and assumptions about children, childhood and children's worlds. It means tuning in to the ways in which people disagree, and, even more importantly, thinking about the *reasons* why they disagree. It means identifying complex and untidy issues, and logically following through and teasing out what different viewpoints might mean. It means always asking 'why?'

The next chapter will help you to see the role of further reading to extend this process of critical enquiry.

2

Reading into Writing

chapter themes

- This chapter will unpack why tutors give you reading lists and will often set particular papers, books or chapters for you to absorb before, during or after teaching sessions. It will help you use them to guide your reading about childhood. The chapter will also show, through worked examples, the ways in which secondary texts are students' windows onto, and access into, an academic, authoritative debate.

Getting to grips with why reading matters so much on CS/ECS degrees

Chapter 1 highlighted that CS/ECS courses explore how views and opinions about children and childhood are not fixed, but will vary according to lots of different factors. However, to do well on your CS/ECS course you will need to be able to think and write academically, not just recognize that everyone sees childhood in different ways. This will involve taking hold not just of the language of academic discourse, but also the range and diversity of ideas, concepts, ideologies and standpoints that exist around childhood. This crucially rests upon a student's *reading*.

Reading is a hugely important activity on any degree course. Once you understand why it is important and can pinpoint what you are trying to achieve by 'reading round' a topic, you will be in a position to develop your own approach to the research that needs to be done in order to write a successful assignment. This chapter offers practical examples of effective reading strategies used by students on their CS/ECS courses and relates them directly to the act of student writing. Above all, by the end of this chapter we hope you'll see that reading and writing are ongoing and integrated aspects of learning, rather than something you must do only at the end of a module when you have to physically produce the assignment.

Learning how to see the significance of the reading that tutors set for you

We said in Chapter 1 that you need to tune in to each tutor's perspective by considering the debates, key questions and issues they highlight in taught sessions. You can also learn a huge amount about how they view the topic from the reading that they ask you to do. It's vital that you engage with this, as it's another crucial aspect of getting to know your tutor and being sure that your work eventually meets their expectations.

Reading lists and the chapters, articles or books set for particular teaching sessions will introduce you to and also immerse you in academic debates about the sorts of ideas and issues that the lecturer wants you to grasp. They will show you a range of theoretical frameworks or approaches or beliefs, any of which can be used as lenses by which to view different aspects of childhood. In short, they will act as a 'toolkit of ideas' which can enable you to perceive different perspectives; compare, contrast and consider the implications of different viewpoints on childhood; and make points yourself when writing about a topic. Tutors will expect you to use these terms and concepts when you prepare your assignment. Let's think about how and why you should invest a lot of time in reading.

In Figure 2.1 you can see how, during their first year, two of our students remember moving from passive to active approaches to learning. To tell you their story they used Comic Life software as a reflective tool (see http://www.plasq.com). You will notice that reading, and talking about different things they had read, played a vital role in their ability to become critical.

Doing the reading in preparation for seminars and teaching sessions

When lecturers set reading that they want you to do before a session, they will typically do so to help you make sense of the literature you need to know about before you can come to understand their topic area. If they say that

Figure 2.1   Going critical with Kim and Dawn. Created using Comic Life (http://plasq.com/comiclife)

reading a specific text is required or essential, they mean it. Such readings are going to be those that offer the greatest insight into a topic. Lecturers will guide you to see the set reading's significance, and help you to perceive the questions and issues raised by reading theory. Don't waste this opportunity – it's your chance to rehearse your ideas and understandings before they 'count' in written assignments. After reading, ask about anything you don't understand, and check for yourself whether you've got the right end of the stick by talking it through with peers and tutors. Discussing your reading with friends allows you to put things into your own words and actively start to make your own sense of important concepts.

In the case study below, for example, is a concrete illustration of how lecturers might use theoretical reading to help you move beyond commonsense views of an issue by encouraging you to *use* (rather than just obtain) theory. This is often what they want you to do in your assignments – so use every chance you have to rehearse this as the module unfolds.

 case study

Perspectives on childhood: comparing theoretical viewpoints

In a key introductory module designed to highlight the range and diversity of different views of the child, students were asked to read two brief extracts, reproduced in the module guide, that were drawn from academic articles. These extracts both discussed the position of the child in the family, but each took a markedly different standpoint, which is precisely why the lecturers had set them for students to consider.

- One outlined Postman's ideas, and was set because it represented 'New Right' ideology, by implicitly assuming that the 'best' family form is middle-class, patriarchal, with two parents and so on. It expressed the view that such family structures are fundamental mechanisms that allow for the protection and preservation of a hallowed form of childhood innocence that children need in order to feel special and flourish.
- The other drew attention to Holt's ideas, who argued that such an outwardly 'perfect' childhood and family life may actually disguise a potentially

(Continued)

27

(Continued)

oppressive childhood experience, in which children may have few rights, are infrequently listened to, and are consigned to a social position of inferiority and limitation, in which they are supposed to appear relentlessly happy. Childhood, according to Holt, might be experienced as a prison, rather than a Romantic garden.

In the teaching session the lecturers assumed that the students had read and reflected on the extracts. They asked students to briefly discuss each theorist's viewpoint in small groups, by comparing and contrasting their perspectives and the way that the articles defined the terms 'child' and 'family'.

Then they asked students to *use and apply* these viewpoints to analyse an extremely conservative photograph of a family, which depicted the father and mother posing with their arms round their two children, a boy (carrying a football) and a girl (carrying a book). Because of their view of childhood and the family, each theorist is likely to interpret aspects of this image differently.

- One is likely to see the father's arm as a protective shield around his child's shoulders, while the other is likely to regard the father's arm as a restraint that is keeping the child in its lowly place.
- One is likely to view the children's neat clothes as a sign of the loving family's care and provision for its children, the other may see the children's clothes as signs of enforced conformity and denial of individual expression, so the children are seen as possessions and showpieces, rather than people with their own views and opinions.
- One might see the gender roles as a mark of natural normality, the other might see them as representing subservience and oppressive forms of dominance and expectation within the family dynamic.

The questions raised by the lecturers in the plenary discussion related to issues of power, choice, autonomy and control. Again, this is an instance in which you can pick up important cues about the themes and issues tutors regard as important – you should tap into them as you develop your assignment. Always ask yourself: what ideas, issues and questions does the lecturer want me to get out of this reading?

What is an argument?

To be able to *use* any given theory, as in the case above, you need to have developed a firm grasp of the main arguments each theorist puts forward or asserts – the big ideas and ways of defining terms. Try to make notes, therefore, which précis or summarize a theorist's arguments – the main way they see things or the 'take' they have on something, their theoretical standpoint. This will often mean 'reading into' what they say and how they say it, because their assumptions might be tacit. For instance, if you were to read Neil Postman's *The Disappearance of Childhood* (1983) you would need to identify his ideological perspective. He doesn't tell you what this is, or that his views could be considered extreme in any way. Instead, he assumes that the reader shares his values, position and statements about 'the family', his analysis of society, children's needs and adults' rights. In short, he argues that childhood is disappearing and highlights why, for him, this is a bad thing, but he does this from his own perspective – his values, attitudes and assumptions. (Our summary can be seen in the first two bullets in the above case study as an example of précising an argument or perspective.)

Note, too, that you're often looking for *sets of ideas* rather than individual people's *personal* views when you are reading. In this case, for example, it wouldn't matter to the lecturer which theorist (specific person) you used when it came to producing your final assignment. Instead, Postman and Holt were simply used at one point as *illustrations* of a particular viewpoint, or as representing a dominant set of ideas about views of the child in the family. You could have used a range of others, as long as they represented diverse views and standpoints. In short, in order to write about the key concepts of any module, you need to be able to summarize and synthesize a whole body of academic writing succinctly.

Keeping good notes by asking yourself questions as you read: reading with a pen and summarizing effectively

Just as it's really unhelpful to simply copy down what someone says in a lecture, it's also not much use just sitting in front of a book. To profit from reading, it's useful to think of it, like Kim and Dawn do in their comic strip (see Figure 2.1), as an activity or conversation, in which you, as well as the writer of the book or article, have an important part to play.

Creating good notes takes time, as it needs to be done slowly and steadily. Making effective notes that summarize the main viewpoint of the theory that you read will ensure that you read for understanding, rather than just gathering mountains of material which you haven't thought about at all. Everyone makes photocopies of articles and chapters, meaning to read them, but then we put them in a file, or under the bed, and forget about them until the assignment is due. Instead, to make sure you don't have to panic or rush, read them and make notes *just after* you copy them, outlining the arguments – the main ideas – and comparing and contrasting them with other things you have read, reading between the lines and highlighting just a few juicy illustrative quotes which you might use to bring your assignment to life. This will also help you to avoid plagiarizing by accident (there is more on this in the next chapter).

Make effective notes by *asking questions* about the material you're going through when reading, by trying to group and categorize perspectives on a topic, rather than just copying chunks out. Scan a chapter or article to get the gist of its perspective, then try and put it in your own words, in a highly selective way, rather than writing reams. Boil it down so you can summarize the main ideas on an index card. Ask yourself 'What are the main ideas?' 'What does this author believe?' 'How does this fit in (or not) with another author's argument?' Summarizing or précising your reading like this is the key to producing a good assignment.

For instance, children's reading of comics and magazines is sometimes a focus in articles and books on literacy. When reading these articles or books, one of the key questions you might ask yourself is whether the writers see comic and magazine reading as a good or bad thing. Further, asking why they think that and whether there are any clues to that in what you read, should help you to establish that there are a number of perspectives here that can be grouped together, ranging from seeing comics as a way of fostering literacy through to undermining it.

If you write down what you find out in response to the questions, thus *doing* something with the information, you're going to have valuable notes that you can use to write your assignment. You're also going to have a set of reminders to yourself about what you don't really understand, which will help you make the most of teaching sessions and tutors. This is what your lecturers want you to do. Let's look at a concrete example of what we mean by this.

 to think about

Reading more about the care and education of young children

Imagine you have been asked, for your assignment, to consider the issues surrounding the question: 'What counts as "quality curricula" in early years education?' You would set out to research (read about) different early years approaches – building on what the teaching sessions covered. In doing your reading, though, you should not set out to gather simply factual information about each of these approaches and then say (describe) what Forest Schools, Reggio Emilia, Portage, Highscope and the Foundation Stage in the UK do. Instead you should think *why* these approaches have developed as they have and what they reveal about the views of children's needs that are embedded within them.

So, what specific questions might you look to answer or address when you're doing this reading research? You might ask, for instance:

- What are the underpinning values, attitudes and beliefs about children's and practitioners' roles and responsibilities on which this curriculum approach is based?
- What factors that impact on children's development are relevant to this curriculum approach?
- What tensions and challenges can you identify in this approach for practice (issues)?

Having specific questions in mind will mean that you read with a purpose. Summarizing each approach in a bank of notes under these headings will help you to perceive the similarities and differences, and possible tensions, between the various perspectives. This is fundamental to you being able to develop an argument in response to the question, which wants you to explore the issue of competing definitions of 'quality' in this context.

 to think about

What do tutors mean by 'defining the terms you use in your essay'?

Another way of looking at this is to consider that in order to write about perspectives on 'quality' you need to be able to define the term 'quality'. A dictionary definition here is simply not good enough, because it will be too broad. What the lecturer actually wants to see is that you have understood that definitions of quality will vary according (in this case) to the different perspectives on education and views of the child that underpin each philosophical approach. The lecturer here expects you to make points about different views of 'quality' – which you can only get by reading further on the topic of early years curricula approaches and reading with a pen.

to think about

Reading further will help you to develop ideas and perceive the issues

If, furthermore, you research different perspectives on a range of curricula approaches you can then begin to ask more complex and sophisticated questions by comparing and contrasting your notes.

Key issues will then begin to emerge from your reading (e.g. views of the child as an apprentice or dependent and unskilled versus the child as an autonomous active learner). Alternatively, your reading may reveal whether a curricular approach incorporates letting children choose how they want to play and what they want to learn about. A further question might then be, 'What "side effects" might the hidden curriculum have?' or 'Is the process of learning actually more influential than the content?' All of these will be answered differently by different philosophies and theorists, relating to views of 'quality' education, and can form the basis of your writing – becoming points to develop, or possible angles you might take on the subject.

We will discuss how to develop the focus for your assignment in the next chapter, but for now it's important to emphasize how reading for understanding is essential, as it establishes the bedrock of your thinking.

Regardless of the original question, a similar range of perspectives or 'lenses' or 'ways' of viewing may well emerge, creating a basic toolkit of ideas useful in most learning situations. Reading enables you to become familiar with this toolkit and also more confident and authoritative in your ability to explore, interpret and recognize controversies and tensions within and between these.

As one student put it, this can be quite different from former reading experiences:

At college, you were given all the criteria, but it's more explicit. I mean – you really can't go wrong. You know all you have to do is put in the things they tell you. If that goes in, then really, you're going to pass. But [at university] it's like, well, you've got the criteria, but you've got to get an angle. You've got to look into it more – much more. It's really affected the way I'm going about reading.

This student now saw reading as a matter of 'looking into' something, rather than gathering things to 'put in'. Students who do well in assignments tend to see the whole business of information literacy in this way – they will try to make sense of what they read and forge it into something new.

Good recording habits when you read: avoiding plagiarism

Along with keeping good notes you should develop the habit of taking down all the bibliographic details of the book that you have been looking at, as the reading lists below do. While there are a number of different ways of doing this most universities use Harvard style (see, for example, http://libweb.anglia.ac.uk/ referencing/harvard.htm). Find out what your university uses and start to write down book details in this format now. It will swiftly become automatic. This means that you will have created a bibliography you can use for your assignment.

Along with the full bibliographic details, make a note of direct quotes that you feel are key ones, with page references (which you will also need for the final assignment). Put these in quotation marks and put your own ideas in something like square brackets, just so that you don't mix them up and accidentally plagiarize.

This advice also applies to the reading you do when visiting websites. The Internet has contributed to a rise in plagiarism because of the sheer volume and immediacy of material and the ease of 'cutting and pasting' from it. Keep details of electronic sources in with your other reading records, including when you viewed the document and the web address. Similarly, put any material you 'cut and paste' in quotation marks to ensure that you don't mix it up with your own ideas.

Finally, keeping these details in one form or another means that you can update it easily as your reading develops. Maintaining records like this means that every bit of reading you do will be remembered, and so can be referred back to for assignments all the way through your degree, whereby nothing is ever wasted. It also allows you to see where you have been, mapping out your journey through academic reading.

'I don't know where to start – there seems to be so much material'

A key difficulty experienced by many students is feeling overwhelmed by the amount of reading material there is in the library, and by the length of the reading lists. The scale of both tells you that reading your way into a topic area is, from the academic's viewpoint, absolutely vital. However, don't panic, or put this reading off. Most people will feel 'lost' at first, so talk to your peers about reading and research, as you can all help one another.

Writing an essay at university is so different! They expect you to use the library, the journals. I'd definitely never done anything like that! At first I was lost, I'd no idea. I didn't know what they expected of me.

Also, take heart – you will learn to read strategically, as well as widely, which will make the reading more manageable. Here, for example, are a couple of experienced students talking about what they try to do when they set about reading:

Student A: I don't read every word any more, but you're trying to pick out key points. You try to figure out what they think.

Student B: I look for someone with the same views as myself. And then I look for someone with a contrasting view.

They are talking about reading with a purpose – looking for different perspectives, as we flag up above. Instead of reading to answer the question, they're reading to quite consciously 'open up more questions'.

I'm finding that it's not straightforward sort of information, it's more opening up areas of interest. For example, at college we took an area of child development, and we did it in the first module at university, but we did it from the view of people I'd never even heard of! Because at college we didn't think about it like that. Here, I'm going to the library and looking at all these books – I've bought books hand over fist! Because as I'm reading I do a comparison, and I've been thinking 'Well, they're all on children's development in school, but that one's dead different to that one!' So it sort of opens up. And then you read the references of one book and it just gets bigger and bigger. Because what I'm trying to do is keep more broad, in an attempt to understand how they compare, or how they oppose each other. And that's changing what I already knew, so that it's changing all the time. That's what I'm trying to do.

This is a very useful thing to do when you're reading – it means you're setting out to try to group or categorize perspectives, as we mentioned above. You can do this by deliberately looking for people who are for and against something, and asking yourself 'on what grounds do they base their views and assumptions?' Once you've found different perspectives and definitions, you can then begin to focus further by analysing the possible reasons for their different outlooks.

Don't forget, too, to check your reading lists for 'key' or 'core' texts. Many lecturers will highlight these because they offer useful overviews of the various debates that are held within their module. Whilst these books may not go into the sort of detail you will eventually be expected to explore, they will give you a valuable introduction to the area, so they are the ones you should read first. Think of them as offering you a map of a country, rather than a town: the scale doesn't let you see the detail – you will need to 'zoom in' on that later as you focus on a particular area you want to explore – but it helps you form a sense of the wider context and the major routes that can be taken. Without doing this sort of background reading, you can easily miss some essential perspectives and approach your assignment too simplistically. It's worth remembering, too, that most academic articles or books will start with a synopsis of the theoretical context to their study – their summaries of the major viewpoints in a particular field – so it's useful to look at a range of opening chapters or introductions when you start any new topic.

Reading into reading lists

When you go to the library, if you do feel swamped by the amount of texts available, make sure you go armed with the reading lists you have been given.

On a straightforward and immediate level you can learn a great deal about a tutor's expectations and outlook on the material simply by skimming the reading list. Compare and contrast the examples below, for instance. You can tell a lot just from the synopsis and the books chosen. It's important to learn to ask yourself key questions about the reading lists to identify a lecturer's particular 'take' on a topic. What is their approach to the subject matter? What discipline are they part of? Which section of the library are these books in? What is their Dewey number? What does the module descriptor suggest are the main ideas of the module?

 worked example

Module title: Studying Childhood and Media

You can tell from this reading list that the tutor is interested in issues to do with the media effects debates, and wants students to explore the ways in which children and young people are regarded as passively consuming or actively interpreting television and other media. The Dewey numbers are largely at the start of the 300s, e.g. 301.16, in the broad area of sociology.

Bazalgette, C. and Buckingham, D. (1995) *In Front of the Children*. London: British Film Institute

Buckingham, D. (1993) *Children Talking Television: The Making of Television Literacy*. London: Falmer Press

(Continued)

(Continued)

Buckingham, D. (1999) *Children's Television in Britain: History, Discourse and Policy*. London: British Film Institute

Buckingham, D. (2000) *After the Death of Childhood: Growing Up in the Age of Electronic Media*. Cambridge: Polity

Gauntlett, D. (2005) *Moving Experiences: Media Effects and Beyond*, 2nd edn. London: John Libbey

Gauntlett, D. (2008) *Media, Gender and Identity: An Introduction*, 2nd edn. London: Routledge

Gauntlett, D. (2009) *Theory.org* [online] Available at: http://www.theory.org.uk/ [Accessed 16 April 2009]

McRobbie, A. (1991) *Feminism and Youth Culture: From Jackie to Just Seventeen*. Basingstoke: Macmillan Education

Robinson, M. (1997) *Children Reading Print and Television*. London: Falmer Press

Seiter, E. (1995) *Sold Separately: Children and Parents in Consumer Culture*. New Brunswick: Rutgers UP

Walkerdine, V. (1999) 'Violent Boys and Precocious Girls: regulating childhood at the end of the millenium'. *Contemporary Issues in Early Childhood*, 1 (1), 3–23

The toolkit of ideas would be about active agency and viewing – children and young people as sense-makers.

 worked example

Module title: Where the Hobgoblins Are

Synopsis: For some children the hobgoblins were real, for others they were fairies and for some they were social issues to be tackled. This unit seeks to use first hand archival material to develop the narrative as seen through the eyes of children in times past.

Indicative reading

History as subject/nature of history

Jordanova, L. (2000) *History in Practice*. London: Arnold

Marwick, A. (2001) *The New Nature of History: Knowledge, Evidence, Language*. Basingstoke: Palgrave

Samuel, R. and Thompson, P. (eds) (1990) *The Myths We Live By*. London: Routledge

Methodology

Fines, J. (1990) *Reading Historical Documents*. Oxford: Blackwell

Context

Long, J. (1999) *Conversations in Cold Rooms: Women Work & Poverty in the 19th Century*. London: Northumberland Royal Historical Society/Boydell Press

Ward, T. and Ward, C. (1991) *Images of Childhood in Old Postcards*. Stroud: Sutton

Narratives

Thompson, T. (1981) *Edwardian Childhood*. London: RKP

Warner, M. (1994) *From Beast to the Blonde: On Fairy Tales and their Tellers*. London: Vintage

Warner, M. (1998) *No Go the Bogeyman: Scaring, Lulling and Making Mock*. London: Vintage

Documents

Newcastle upon Tyne Archive Materials

You can tell from this reading list that:

- the main approach to subject matter is historical – the lecturer is keen to introduce students to historical ways of approaching and researching childhood.
- checking the catalogue shows that these texts are shelved in Dewey number 704 (folklore, fear, devils and monsters); and Dewey number 930 (different histories – women, oral, memory, history-philosophy).
- the lecturer is interested in narratives and representations of childhood in the past, with the different versions of stories that were told.
- the main ideas are around the relative nature of representation and who controls and tells the stories. This is the toolkit of ideas.
- finally, the lecturer takes students to research primary material based in archives (e.g. school records) to see if and how children's voices are present and how children are viewed and recorded in this material.

 worked example

Module title: An Introduction to Safeguarding Children

In this module students will have the opportunity to develop their awareness of the legislative, professional and societal context in which safeguarding services operate.

(Continued)

(Continued)

Reading list

Allen, N. (2005) *Making Sense of the Children Act 1989*, 4th edn. Chichester: John Wiley and Sons Ltd

Barker, R. (ed) (2009) *Making Sense of Every Child Matters: Multi-professional Practice Guidance*. Bristol: Policy Press

Calder, M. (ed) (2004) *Child Sexual Abuse and the Internet: Tracking the New Frontier*. Lyme Regis: Russell House

Calder, M. and Hackett, S. (2003) *Assessment in Child Care: Using and Developing Frameworks for Practice*. Lyme Regis: Russell House

Connolly, M., Crichton-Hill, Y. and Ward, T. (2006) *Culture and Child Protection: Reflective Responses*. London: Jessica Kingsley

Corby, B. (2005) *Child Abuse: Towards a Knowledge Base*, 3rd edn. Buckingham: Open University Press

Farnfield, S. (2008) 'Theoretical model for the assessment of parenting', *British Journal of Social Work*, 38, 1076–1099

Humphreys, C., Mullender, A., Thiara, R. and Skamballis, A. (2006) '"Talking to my mum". Developing communication between mothers and children in the aftermath of domestic violence', *Journal of Social Work*, 6 (1), 53–63

Jones, A. (2003) 'Reconstructing the stepfamily: Old myths, new stories', *Social Work*, 48 (2), 228–237

London, K., Bruck, M., Ceci, S.J. and Shuman, D.W. (2005) 'Disclosure of child sexual abuse: what does the research tell us about the ways children tell?', *Psychology, Public Policy and Law*, 11 (1), 194–226

Nicolson, P. and Wilson, R. (2004) 'Is domestic violence a gender issue? Views from a British city', *Journal of Community and Applied Social Psychology*, 14, 266–283

Parton, N. (2006) *Safeguarding Children: Early Intervention and Surveillance in a Late Modern Society*. Basingstoke: Palgrave Macmillan

From this reading list you can see that the module requires students to stand back and think about their own stance in relation to the underlying philosophical, psychological and sociological perspectives and issues in relation to safeguarding. The texts are in different sections of the library and the toolkit of ideas prompts reflection about whose responsibility safeguarding is.

Why reference?

Having read a wide range of books, how will you be using them in assignments? Primarily, they will appear as references and citations. The requirement to reference your work may be a new one and can be daunting, as this student remembers:

We were never told at college how to reference journals. That bit terrified me.

However, to do well in your assignments you *do* need to refer to a wide range of secondary reading, again emphasizing how important reading is.

This is linked to the way that tutors will look for a reasoned and balanced argument in your assignments. Referencing is part of this as it shows that all the comments you make are qualified ('backed up' and 'substantiated' are other common terms tutors will use) and that you appreciate that issues can be viewed from different perspectives.

The way to support your reasoned and balanced argument in academic writing is to reference 'evidence', 'support' or 'perspectives', as the examples of academic writing in the key point below imply.

 **key point**

General conversation	Academic writing
'It stands to reason'	'The evidence would suggest ...'
'Everyone would agree'	'There is extensive support for ...'
'It is blatantly obvious'	'There is considerable evidence to support the
'It's clear to me'	view ...'
'Children need ...'	'In conclusion, my personal perspective on this
	issue would be ...'

This 'evidence' is some of the material gleaned from your reading. In your own work, then, a wide reading of reliable and authoritative texts is demonstrated by incorporating into the body of the assignment, summaries of the ideas these contain and direct illustrative quotations. This is when you will use citation or 'people in brackets' (of which more in the next chapter) – a conventional way of demonstrating the theoretical reading you have done.

Evidence and authority

Of course, as we suggest above, it does matter *what* you read, too. Some sources will be more reliable and esteemed than others and you will have to be very aware of this when gathering your evidence. The following example as to why some sources can be regarded as more authoritative than others illustrates the point in everyday terms.

to think about

Imagine you're trying to decide where to go on holiday. You've decided you want somewhere warm, for two weeks and you're on a fixed budget. Where would you go/who would you ask to help you decide where to go? How reliable would this evidence be? What would give it authority? In what ways might it be unreliable?

In this example it's quite easy to see that some of the people you could consult will know less or be more biased than others. But telling the difference between a useful academic source and one that is less so can be more challenging. To give you some more pointers, consider the difference between these two statements:

> Children deserve the best in life, and their parents should buy them good books.

and

> ... definitions are controlled by their purpose. There can be, therefore, no single definition of "Children's Literature". What is regarded as a "good" book might be "good" in the sense in which the currently dominant/ literary/academic establishment prescribes; "good" in terms of effectiveness for education, language acquisition, or socialisation or for entertainment for a specific child or group of children in general or specific circumstances; or "good" in some moral or political sense; or "good" in a therapeutic sense. "Good" as an abstract and "good for" as a practical application are constantly in conflict in judgements about children's literature. (Hunt, 1994, pp. 42–43)

The first statement is very sweeping and takes a lot of things and values for granted, while the second shows that definitions of 'good' literature for children will vary according to purpose, thereby problematizing definitions of 'good' and definitions of 'childhood'. In scholarly terms, the second is much better, and, if included in your assignment, evidences authoritative wider reading.

It is also important that you look out for bias. Think about who produced what you are reading at any given point. For example, government-produced websites on policy, like those for Every Child Matters, the Early Years Foundation Stage or the National Curriculum, will be different from academic articles critiquing and unpacking them, or research which explores and evaluates what happens when the rhetoric is put into practice. Obviously the latter will help you engage more fully with the sorts of ideas and questions you've been studying on CS/ECS.

So, when you read, ask another set of questions, ones that focus on the relative authority of your sources. We need to think about what we read, rather than just 'put it in'. These will include a consideration of the expected audience for the source, the purpose and possible bias of the writing, its level of scholarship (there are differences between newspaper articles and academic texts, for instance), its historical and political position, the background of the author and so on.

Some good questions are:

- What is the topic?
- Who wrote it?
- When was it written?
- Why was it written?
- Who was it written for?
- How is it presented?
- How did I react to it?

These questions are useful whether you are working with books or websites. However, there are specific issues when thinking about authority in relation to websites, where understanding how to distinguish reliable sources from unreliable ones is also crucial, as is appreciating how to use and reference material that is effectively 'live' and so is capable of changing daily, unlike a book.

A key approach is to prioritize your own university library electronic resources, which will include information about academic databases and the e-journals selected to support your studies and assignments. The university will direct you to subject specific sites and search engines where you will be able to search for materials in your area. There are also other organizations which have the same function, such as Intute (http://www.intute.ac.uk/about.html) and search engines which have academic user groups in mind, such as Google Scholar (http://scholar.google.co.uk/). In addition, through your university website you are likely to be offered electronic tutorials on developing your skills. Use them to build up your confidence.

When reading material found beyond that suggested on the module reading lists or the university information resources site, remember to ask yourself the questions listed above. Also keep in mind that the further away you 'browse' or 'surf' from known and trusted sources and sites, the more skilled you will need to be in making judgments about the authenticity and reliability of the pages you visit.

In addition, also ask yourself about the address of the site, whether it is an academic institution or another kind of organization. Usually, the existence of '.ac' in the address will clue you into the fact that a site is probably appropriate for your purposes. The example given above in the Worked Example on 'Studying Childhood and Media' however, has '.org' in the address which means you will need to not simply look at the address to get an idea of 'authority'. This is also shown by the website of one of the authors of this book, which can be found at http://www.dr-mel-comics.co.uk/. It also lacks the authority of '.ac'.

When examined more closely, and by asking the questions above, the reader can see the former was developed as part of a university and the latter as a stand-alone site. This gives the former authority. Following through the questions, looking more closely again, shows that both are run by academics who give information about their research. Both are regularly updated and so are current and relevant. Finally, they are aimed at students and lecturers, as well as being attractive to general readers. Depending on the subject, either could prove useful in an assignment. Through asking the questions above, you will be able to develop your skills about the authority of sites.

So, how might these questions work out in practice when looking at written sources? In the following case study, the students were asked to read two extracts illustrating different ways of writing about the topic of parenting education or support, and to apply the questions above.

 case study

Extract 1

Parenting education: report on findings

Academics at Northumbria University have recently published findings from work they have carried out with parents in the North East of England who have all received support from parenting educators.

In total, 37 parents drawn from different backgrounds and with children with a range of ages and difficulties were interviewed by the two researchers, Dr Kay Sambell and Sue Miller, both Senior Lecturers in Childhood Studies and Care and Education. The parents were asked to talk about the different types of challenges that they had experienced in their parenting careers and the kinds of parenting education that they had received.

The authors report that all the parents, regardless of their backgrounds, family situation or social position, spoke of parenting as having been one of, if not the, most challenging task they had ever undertaken. 'What emerged' say the authors 'was a picture of parents often casting around for advice and guidance, adopting trial and error approaches and wanting to do a good job, often against considerable odds. The definition of what counted as "good parenting" appeared to be influenced by trends or fashions which, in turn, highlighted the different perspectives that have existed throughout history of what children's lives "should" be like. Today, factors such as avoiding teenage pregnancy, doing well in school, or having a well paid job, are more likely to be seen as indicators of a child having had good parents than they might have been in the past or in other cultures even today.'

They continue: 'Our views of children are constantly changing and parents today are not always able to turn even to their own parents for advice, either because they are living in a different community and almost certainly because the norms and expectations of today are at some variance from those of the previous generation. Many parents spoke of the enormous support they had received from being able to discuss and reflect on their parenting situation with other parents and parent educators and to find ways of developing close and meaningful relationships with their children that they could individualise to their own situation.'

The report is published as Miller, S. and Sambell, K. (2003) 'What do parents feel they need? Implications of parents' perspectives for the facilitation of parenting programmes'. *Children & Society,* 17(1), 32–44.

Extract 2

Out of control kids: who is to blame?

Do parents need to take more responsibility for their children? How much is too much state help? Should the government do more to teach parenting skills to mums and dads or even make them attend special classes if their children are causing trouble in the community?

(Continued)

(Continued)

Jenny, 15, is the mother of Danny, 3 months. The teachers at her school want her parents to go to their parenting class to learn to be better parents. 'I didn't really know what I was letting myself in for' the high school drop out, sporting nose ring and designer t-shirt, sighed when interviewed. 'No one really tells you about sex at school, and my parents were always too embarrassed. My mum just said "Be careful" and more or less left me to find out about the facts of life from my friends and magazines. She had me when she was 17 and she's done alright.'

Jenny is thinking about going back to school to do some examinations. Thanks to local Labour controlled council policy, she has the right to a free place at the nursery near her home where her baby will be cared for by fully qualified staff alongside other children whose working parents pay up to £150 a week for the privilege. 'There's no way I could afford to use this nursery if the Council didn't support me,' she said. 'Maybe I can get somewhere to live on my own with Danny. My friends told me you can usually get priority if you're a teenage parent.'

Jenny's mother, Terri, 35, unemployed, lives with her partner John, also unemployed, and 3 children: Jordan (11), Kylie (8) and Jake (6). All the children have learning and behavioural difficulties. The school they attend want both parents to have help and to attend their parenting group where they can be taught some of the basics in how to bring up their children to be responsible citizens for the future.

Extract 1 is in the style of a broadsheet newspaper's overview of an academic report. It is supposed to take a broader perspective, to present the issue dispassionately, cite evidence for the assertions it makes, appear non-judgmental and logically structured. It is a cooler, more objective style of writing, which uses less emotive language and more complicated words, phrases and sentences.

Extract 2 is done in a tabloid journalism style – it makes sweeping generalizations, is opinionated and judgmental (talks of 'better' parents), draws upon 'commonsense', intuitive notions (e.g. 'I was treated like this as a kid and it's never done me any harm') and displays prejudice ('Terri, 35, unemployed, lives with her partner John' ... the implication being a train of thinking which concludes that 'no wonder the kids have problems'). The piece has a hidden agenda: it attempts to appeal to our feelings and connect with us as individuals, focusing on the individual person by quoting an individual child and mother. It is written in a subjective and campaigning style; and its main weakness is that it presents only one, exaggerated side of the story, which tries to close down debate and lure you into agreement. Be on your guard for devices like these. You need to develop the ability to read critically like this, so, as a starting point, you can practise spotting these for yourself in most tabloid stories about children and childhood.

On one level the broadsheet style is something to emulate in your writing and reading, especially at first. One student showed he was getting the right idea when he said:

> *That little exercise [above] was good, because it helped you to start thinking 'Well, what's this writer trying to say?' And I've been doing that now when I read books. And also it shows you what to look for when you're writing your-self. I think about having an argument differently now – I think of it as hav-ing something to say, and different viewpoints, rather than getting at someone, trying to shoot them down. And when I did my assignments, it really helped, because I tried to ask questions about where the articles were coming from, rather than just telling them what the article said. I saw that's what they wanted me to do.*

Remember, though, how important it is to *read widely* to inform writing, to incorporate evidence, balance and authority in your work. This is where the broadsheet-style article misses out – it's not sufficiently scholarly in its for-mat or presentation to be handed in as an assignment. It does not, for instance, summarize different theoretical viewpoints in an overview of the area, as an academic piece of writing does.

Although the broadsheets point the way to more formal and academic kinds of writing, they do not go far enough. You need to develop an academic way of writing that is different from everyday talking and thinking, and reading academic books and journals is the only way of learning how to do this. It takes practice and feels very unfamiliar, but again, you can only learn by doing it.

Reading to get an angle on your essay

All of the points above, however, do not mean that you can't use tabloid or broadsheet stories as *inspirations* for research, or to help you focus your assignment. Here's a student talking about just that:

> *I look for controversies in newspapers – that gets me started asking ques-tions, which I then follow up in the library. Like, for instance, I got the idea of doing smacking on the Children's Rights module, because there was an article on it in the papers.*

Learning to use the appropriate terminology

Reading strategically is also essential on a module-by-module basis as you will need to familiarize yourself with the specific terminology each lecturer uses, because this, for them, becomes shorthand for big ideas and concepts. It takes a while to immerse oneself in the terminology – but it also gets easier with time. You need to build up statement and word banks, based on the specific vocabulary or terminology you will hear in lectures and find in the required reading, which will then help you to develop and express an appropriate argument when writing the final assignment for a particular module. For instance, in the lectures given in relation to the module 'Studying Childhood and Media' mentioned earlier, key terms would include 'the active viewer', 'media effects' and 'constructions of childhood'.

Reading into writing

To highlight the vital importance of academic reading we will now present several short worked examples of a number of different student responses to the writing task 'What do you understand by the term "the social construction of childhood"?' We will discuss how these would achieve a range of grades, and we will offer explanations of the strengths and weaknesses in each, specifically concentrating on the ways in which they evidence each student's ability to summarize and represent the important ideas they have been studying. You will see how and why wider reading is vital.

 worked example

What do you understand by the term 'the social construction of childhood'?

Answer 1

My understanding of the social construction of childhood is as follows. Childhood can be seen as the period in a young person's life between dependence and independence. It may be represented as a fact of human life, with biology determining a dependency on others to provide care.

Whilst immaturity and dependence may be biological facts of life, James and Prout (1990) contend that 'The way in which this immaturity is understood and made meaningful is a fact of culture' (p. 7).

They suggest that facts of culture may vary, and this can be said to make childhood a social construction. In this sense childhood is not a static, objective and universal fact of human nature, but a social construction that is both culturally and historically determined. Comparative analysis actually reveals a variety of childhoods, rather than a single, universal, cultural phenomenon. The nature of childhood varies according to the ways in which it is interpreted and different meanings are attached to it.

James, A. and Prout, A. (eds) (1990) *Constructing and Reconstructing Childhood: Contemporary Issues in the Sociological Study of Childhood*. London: Falmer Press.

Answer 2

It is very difficult to define the various social constructions of childhood. However, James and Prout define this as a 'shifting social and historical construction' (James and Prout, 1990).

Some theorists suggest that social constructions are linked to race, culture, gender, class and time. Some of the key social constructions are:

- Children as persons in their own right
- Children as innocent
- Children as vulnerable
- Children as members of a distinct group
- Children as apprentices
- Children as animals.

Answer 3

The social construction of childhood is build up of a variety of different theories. I feel that the environment that the child is surrounded by and the time when the child is growing up can influence the child.

Our society treats boys and girls very differently. We treat girls like they are very delicate and precious and that they need protecting from the world. With boy's we believe that they are rough and rouged and they should do the protecting. If that's the messages of our society, children behave like that. They are social constructed.

Answer 1 would receive the best mark – promising to be in the 2:1 range. It offers a summary of the term based on wider reading and is properly referenced. It shows that the student is, via relevant reading, beginning to grasp the important key concepts, key terms and theoretical constructs, which are lacking in Answer 3, which seems to have 'just been written' without secondary reading. If there has been any reading, in Answer 3 it has clearly been of books in a totally different field, and the lecturer might wonder if the student has confused social construction theory with the very different concept of socialization. The assessor of this work would probably suspect that the student was dimly recalling 'A' level Sociology (or had looked up 'socialization' in a dictionary and not realized it was different). He might bristle at being included in the sweeping and unsubstantiated statement 'we treat girls ...'. The spelling and other mistakes also suggest that it has not been proofread. All of these things indicate that the student hasn't really read round sufficiently to understand the central concepts of that module. The work would receive a low mark or possible fail, because of its central misunderstanding.

In comparison, Answer 2 is much more coherent and shows evidence of some reading, but it is less focused and less accomplished at summarizing the reading than Answer 1, so more likely to achieve a mark in the 2:2 range. It contains a list of bullet points that should be presented as a quotation, as the student has actually copied down Mills and Mills' (2000) categories, without citing the source. Lecturers will know the field so well that they will spot this and the student will want to avoid them thinking that they were trying to pass off Mills and Mills' ideas as their own. In your own case lecturers will be pleased that you have read thus far, but you must take care to cite *all* the reading sources that you draw directly upon. It's best to include a list of references as in Answer 1, even for the shortest piece of writing. Furthermore, 'putting in' bullet points as we see in Answer 2 leaves the reader having to make sense of what they read, rather than the writer explaining what they are to understand.

In summary, then, the extracts illustrate the differences between 'commonsense', personal, opinionated writing, and that based on wider academic reading – what we call 'reading into writing'.

3

Producing a Good Assignment

 chapter themes

- You now know that going to lectures and reading over a period of time are fundamental to producing a good assignment on CS/ECS. This chapter, though, concentrates on making sure that you actually display your learning to its best advantage when it comes to handing in an assignment.
- On CS/ECS degrees you will be assessed, for the most part, via coursework of different kinds, so in this chapter we talk extensively about the process of producing good written assignments and managing your time effectively. In addition, this chapter gives guidance on exams and on what to do if things go wrong.

Getting the basics right

It is important to create the right impression when producing an assignment. Your work should look professional, and have an academic and scholarly tone similar to the authoritative texts that you've read.

With regard to layout and style, always check with tutors in case your university has particular preferences. Whether subheadings are considered appropriate varies from place to place, as does whether you can use the first person. Make sure you follow any departmental requirements too (e.g. if front sheets are needed or if you should just print on one side of the paper) so that you don't throw marks away. The list below should help to guide you.

- **Do not include any pictures on the front cover of your assignment** and especially no Clipart images of toddlers on tricycles. This is not appropriate.
- **Make sure that the information on the front cover is clear and thorough.** Include your name and student number and other relevant information.
- **The title should be clear.** If you have a set question, use that as the title. Alternatively if you can choose your own angle on a question, consider using a subtitle, e.g. a title like 'It's all very well to say you'll act in the best interests of the child, until you come to put that into practice. Discuss with reference to a specific context of your own choosing' might be more clearly represented as, 'It's all very well to say you'll act in the best interests of the child, until you come to put that into practice. An exploration of parents' and teachers' views of "best practice" for children with special educational needs', as this subtitle directs the assessor into your particular 'take' on the assignment.
- **Use an appropriate font in 12 point.** Times New Roman unless otherwise specified.
- **Number pages consecutively** just in case the secure fastening on your assignment breaks.
- **Leave wide enough margins and line spacing** (1.5–2.0 in the latter case) for the assessor to read your work easily and add comments.
- **Don't use document wallets or bulky cardboard files.** They are awkward to get work in and out of, and posting them to external examiners is difficult, especially if a number need to be sent.
- **Use side-headings as signposts to help your reader.** If you are not allowed to use subheadings, try using them to structure your work in draft form and then take them out before you hand the work in.
- **Bibliography and references** should follow the pattern that your university suggests (probably Harvard style). University websites will include guidance on this, for example, http://www.leedsmet.ac.uk/lskills/open/sfl/content/harvard/. They may also offer tutorial support, for example, http://www.northumbria. ac.uk/sd/central/library/help/skillsplus/.
- **Stick to the word length.**

Drawing on and presenting your wider reading in assignments

What you hand in must show evidence of wider reading. There are some sophisticated ways of doing this, but first we'll show you some basic ways of how you can present your wider reading when you come to write your assignment.

Citation: How to refer to others' work in the text of your assignment

When you introduce a theorist avoid the following:

'A quote is ...'

or

'Berry Mayall wrote the following reference ...'

Try instead to include 'people in brackets', using academic citation techniques:

According to Kehily (2008, p. 5) 'The idea that childhood innocence should be preserved is a pervasive one and can be seen to operate on many levels.'

or, alternatively:

'The idea that childhood innocence should be preserved is a pervasive one and can be seen to operate on many levels' (Kehily, 2008, p. 5).

Quotation marks are essential when using an author's actual words in the order they said them, i.e. if you directly quote them. When you do this you also need to include a reference to the page they said the words on. All the other bibliographic information should be put in the list of references you include at the *end* of your assignment (the bibliography).

Instead of quoting Kehily directly, though, you could summarize her views as follows:

Kehily (2008) argues that the concept of childhood innocence, as a state to be preserved, is persistent and might function on many levels.

Because you have not directly cited her words you don't need to include the page reference, but using Kehily (2008) in the sentence means it's clear these are her views, put into your own words.

Don't use too many quotes. Instead, make points in your own words, as above, and only use direct quotes occasionally, to 'back up' the point with an example.

Useful statement bank

The following ways of expressing and analysing your reading might also be useful:

Kehily (2008) suggests ... asserts ... outlines ... puts forward the view that ... assumes ... believes ... points out ... conjectures ... claims ... upholds the idea that ... contests ... states ... maintains ... observes ... emphasizes ... stresses ... highlights ... contends ... supports the view that ... .

The following ways of expressing and analysing your reading might be useful, too:

[X's] ... model/philosophy/conceptual framework/ideals/beliefs/attitude/ thinking/ideas/proposals/approach ... seem(s) based upon the ... hypothesis/ theory/assumption/conjecture/presumption/premise/opinion/supposition/ idea ... that [children need ...]

Beware misquoting

This is from a student essay:

> A quote from the book Childhood *written by Chris Jenks says* Childhood is *conventionally seen as a time of carefree disorganized bliss ... The bliss goes that they [children] enjoy non-serious, play-directed activities. They avoid work and serious activities at all costs ...*

Firstly, the reference is missing: it should be (Jenks, 1996). Secondly, Jenks didn't actually say all of this, or at least, the bits he did say are not in quotation marks with the page number included. The student has either misinterpreted, or copied it down wrongly. Further, it's unclear when the student starts talking and Jenks stops. Good records and note-taking should prevent this.

Avoid lists of rhetorical questions

The following student wrote:

> *The word childhood presents problems, are we talking about a boy or a girl? How old are they? How long does childhood last in terms of age? 0–10? 0–14? 0–18?*

She has identified key problems of definition, and is aware of the questions surrounding the definition of the word 'childhood', but needs to rephrase her questions in a more authoritative manner. A better way of expressing the same thing might be:

> *Defining the term 'childhood' is complex. Some definitions focus on age specificity, but there is little agreement about which ages are relevant. Other complications include diverse cultural factors and biological and social determinants, such as gender.*

Always acknowledge sources: avoiding plagiarism (revisited)

This student wrote:

So what is the phenomenon of childhood itself? Is it a state of powerlessness? Or maybe a condition of secrets and shame? Is the child an innocent creature? Are children in need of protection from the adult world? Is it a period of dependency? Or maybe a period of biological, intellectual and social development?

Bits of this sound like they have come from further reading rather than being the student's own ideas and words. As nobody else is formally acknowledged, the tutor might worry about plagiarism, which is like 'kidnapping' other people's work or inspiration without taking care to indicate where the text has come from (there is more on avoiding this in the previous chapter in the section 'Good recording habits when you read: avoiding plagiarism'). In this instance it may be accidental, but acknowledging the source of your ideas via references is a fundamental aspect of academic writing. So make sure you include your 'people in brackets' by keeping accurate records when reading and consistently using the Harvard author (date) convention in your assignment writing. Such citation is seen as a sign of wider reading, strength and plain good manners, as it helps you show that you are not passing off someone else's work as your own.

Plagiarism includes summarizing your reading without saying where it came from; drawing on other people's ideas, concepts or theories without stating whose ideas they are; or using words in pretty much the way they were used in the original text you accessed. You *must* avoid cutting and pasting in chunks from material you have accessed online. It is often seen as straightforward cheating if students do this and there is software which detects this type of direct copying. In fact, many universities now enable you to use online detection systems, such as TurnitinUK, to obtain an originality report for your draft assignment, so that you can check what percentage of your work matches other texts held in the database before hand-in. This helps you avoid plagiarism.

Remember, though, tutors really want to see your line of thought – the argument – in your writing. So don't simply give them unrelated strings of other people's ideas, even if they are suitably acknowledged, as this will get low marks, because it is a passive approach. Nor should you just give them back their lecture: lectures are just the springboard for your own study and besides, lecturers know what they think – they want to hear your ideas. Never put (Kay Sambell, Powerpoint lecture, 2009) as a reference: you *must* read round the topic.

Rather than simply describing (or 'putting in') what you have read, try to *make points* about its significance. Identify connections between different perspectives you have encountered, comparing and contrasting elements of your reading, so that you are acting like an author and not like a parrot who purely repeats back what's been said before. Try to create your own structure, rather than copying the ways in which material is structured in the things you read. Further, use quotations sparingly and accurately in your assignments.

The main way of avoiding plagiarism (and, incidentally, becoming an active learner) is, however, to develop your own academic 'voice'. This means getting into the habit of using your own words *all the time,* not just in your assignments. When you make notes, put them in your own words, rather than copying out long chunks from articles, cutting and pasting, photocopying or taking lecture notes verbatim. Before you start your assignment, practise informally by 'teaching' someone else about what you have read, as it will help you rehearse the ideas by speaking them aloud in your own words, and allow you check the extent to which you have really grasped the material you are studying. If you do this, you are, in effect, giving yourself a 'dry-run' at summarizing the main ideas and outlining different viewpoints on themes and issues when you come to write your assignment. In this way you will avoid simply repeating stuff unthinkingly.

The students writing above are, however, on the right lines – they can perceive key questions and issues, and recognize the 'it depends' nature of knowledge. Nonetheless, the writing they handed in would have been greatly improved by using 'people in brackets' effectively.

Setting out your references via a bibliography at the end of your assignment

Only include authors to whom you have actually referred as a 'person in brackets' in the body of your essay and list the references alphabetically. This is so that anyone interested in your discussion of Jenks (1996) can easily find all the details they need to order his book for themselves, by skimming the references at the end of your essay. Putting all these details in the body of your work would interrupt the flow of your writing, which is why we use the author (date) convention.

The first example is annotated, simply to help you understand what all the information means (you don't need to do this).

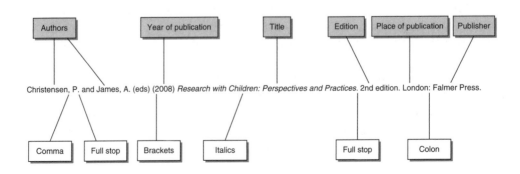

Fumoto, H. and Robson, S. (2006) 'Early Childhood Professionals' Experience of Time to Facilitate Children's Thinking'. *European Early Childhood Education Research Journal*, 14(2), 97–111.

Jenks, C. (1996) *Childhood*. London: Routledge.

National Children's Bureau Current policy issues. Available at: http://www.ncb.org.uk/ [Accessed 1 June 2009].

Sambell, K., Miller, S. and Hodgson, S. (2001) 'Let's Get the Assessment to Drive the Learning', in Schwartz, P. and Webb, G. (eds) *Assessment: Case Studies, Experience and Practice in Higher Education*, pp. 137–143. London: Kogan Page.

Another example of guidance in this is given at http://www.bournemouth. ac.uk/library/citing_references/docs/Citing_Refs.pdf (scroll down to the section entitled 'References at the end of a piece of work').

A lot of students ask 'How many references should I put in?' There are no rules about this. Generally, though, tutors would be disappointed to see only one or two, but, by the same token, won't be duped if you've put lots in but not referred to them in a constructive and illuminative way in your writing.

Avoid final, absolute language: sounding cautious

Use speculative language when writing your assignment. This shows that you realize that the definitions you've drawn on in your wider reading are relative and provisional. By incorporating secondary reading in the following way, you show these are not your personal ideas, but traceable to a range of sources. This helps you achieve an academic, theorized tone while comparing and contrasting the secondary reading. For example,

> Sambell (2009) and Gibson (2010) both suggest that [x]. On the other hand, Miller (2007) puts forward the opposite view, asserting that [y].

Furthermore, by talking about your sources or theorists in a speculative way, you'll avoid falling into the trap of sounding like you think one is right and the other wrong. For instance, you could write

- The differences between the two standpoints might be traced to ...
- Possible ways of explaining these differences lie in ...
- It could be suggested that these views differ because ...
- Potential explanations for the discrepancies between these viewpoints include ...

Editing and proof-reading

Writing an assignment is a long, ongoing process, but another straightforward aspect of getting the basics right lies in careful editing and proof-reading in the later stages. It's useful to have someone else comment on your ideas, plans and drafts. If nothing else, they will help you spot careless errors and typos. In a moment we will turn to discuss time management and suggestions for breaking down assignment writing into clear steps, but for now the important thing to realize is the need to allow ample time, not to hurry, and to allow work time to lie fallow. Sometimes, coming back to it fresh after a little while working on something else will allow you to see it with new eyes and realize more fully its strengths and limitations, enabling you to edit it more effectively.

It is also useful to write the introduction last. This might not sound logical, but when marking, tutors will often initially skim an essay before going through it thoroughly. At this point they will look at the introduction, conclusion, subheadings, the list of references and the title to see where the student is coming from. Writing the introduction last, then, gives the reader an adequate gist of what your argument is. Read back over your work. What have you actually written about? How can you best explain the work, clearly and pithily, in the introduction?

A hurried assignment will probably be structured and worded poorly, as you won't have had a chance to hone and refine it. Further, a piece of work handed in after writing it the night before is guaranteed to be filled with all sorts of errors. Using a spell-checker helps, but it won't notice when you have spelt the word right, but have used the wrong word. Do re-read your assignments.

What to do if life gets in the way

Stuff happens. It may mean that you can't meet your deadline for an assignment. Don't panic, but do let people know. Contact the person in charge of the module for which you cannot hand in the work first. Email them and make an appointment if necessary. They will be able to tell you if you can have an extension (allowing you more time to finish the work) and what forms you might need to fill in, or what proof tutors will need you to provide (e.g. a letter from your GP).

If things are more serious and you are really struggling with *all* your work, then, if you have a personal tutor, they should be your main point of contact. Don't let a problem build up. Don't feel you are alone. Tutors will help with module leaders and forms, or may refer you on to the person in charge of your degree if you need to re-sit a semester or even a year's worth of work.

Finally, you can also contact student services. There are usually sections on the university website. These can offer a huge range of learning and writing support, from how best to approach certain assignments through to helping you with regard to a learning disability. They can also advise you about other issues, such as finance, accommodation and child care.

Structuring and planning your essay

By now you should be clear about how to get the basics right, so let's turn to the most challenging aspects of producing assignments. Effective assignments are organized, focused, develop a *well-founded argument* based on well-assimilated wider reading, and *explore* issues. Weak assignments are ill focused, try to cover too much material, or just gather information to 'put in'. Worse still are those that are untheorized, opinionated and jumbled.

As you read on you will see that essay planning is *much* more complex than simply ensuring you have a beginning, middle and a conclusion.

Don't leave writing your assignment to the last minute

Time management is essential here. The bigger picture is that you will have a number of assignments to complete, and probably domestic and other commitments as well. At the start of each semester, create a chart or diary of what needs to be handed in and when, and factor in any other commitments.

You could combine this with the following breakdown of activities. This shows how to plan your work, from receiving an essay title at the start of term, to the hand-in date, usually 10–12 weeks later (sometimes longer, if holidays are included).

- Unpacking the assignment title.
- Relating information covered in teaching sessions to the title.
- Following up on reading set in lectures.
- Searching relevant websites for information.
- Talking to the tutor about the assignment.
- Discussing ways of tackling the assignment with other students.
- Planning your assignment.
- Doing a first draft.
- Sharing your draft with a colleague and receiving feedback.
- Editing and proof-reading your second draft.
- Checking all references against departmental conventions/referencing guidelines.

Unpacking the assignment title

Be very clear about what you're being asked to do, because planning your response to an assignment question starts here. This links back to getting to know what your tutor is really after and making sure you meet their particular requirements – explicit and implicit.

 case study

Worked example: children's rights

If the assignment title is 'It's all very well saying that you aim to do things in the child's best interests, until you come to put this into practice. Discuss, with reference to a particular context of your own choosing' on a module which has explored childhood and human rights, ask yourself what the tutor is *really* getting at.

If, for example, the module has explored the tensions between different perspectives by asking you to debate tensions between protectionist as opposed to liberationist views of the child then the tutor is *really* asking you

- to theorize definitions/views of 'the child' and, hence, constructions of children's 'needs' and 'best interests'
- to explore how these might impact on different stakeholders' views of 'best interest'
- to identify and highlight the tensions and challenges of operationalizing policy (e.g. the UN convention).

They want you

- to show that you realize that 'it depends': that the tensions relate to who makes the decisions in relation to notions of inclusion and integration
- to unpack views, for and against, and compare and contrast them in a theorized and well-read manner
- to locate your discussion in a specific area/context, such as the smacking debate, children's clothes and uniforms, outdoor play or special education.

To build up a clear view of this, you should relate the teaching sessions to the title, look at any set reading, and talk to peers and tutors about the assignment. This will be done over several weeks, and emphasizes, once again, that you need to get to know your tutor via their lecturing and handouts, as well as from discussions with them.

case study

Worked example: children's literature

The assignment title is: '"Filth, which ever way you look at it": discuss the depiction of teenage sexual activity in Burgess's (2003) controversial novel for young readers, *Doing It'*.

Here the tutor is *really* asking you

- about the different perspectives on the perceived value of children's books
- to provide an analysis of the *reasons* why advocates of Burgess like his book, as opposed to the *reasons* opponents hold for disliking it.

They want you

- to draw on theoretical models from your secondary reading.

This example shows that reading/research for this title need not necessarily be about Burgess's book, but *should* be about theoretical writing which explains the different ways in which literature can be valued. Here wider reading helps create a framework for discussion and also helps you articulate the issues that the essay title is getting at.

As the case studies show, an effective assignment tends to draw, albeit implicitly, on a wide range of research. It also draws on your understanding of the concepts that inform the whole module, rather than 'just' material that directly relates to the specific topic the essay title mentions.

What if you get to choose your own title?

Even if everyone has to respond to the same question, there isn't one 'correct' answer, and you will need your own 'angle' or focus. But sometimes you will get to choose your focus entirely. If so, it is crucial to think about the learning outcomes, assessment criteria and what we said about 'getting to know your tutor' when deciding what to write about. For instance:

worked example

What if, in relation to the children's literature module above, instead of a specific title on Burgess's *Doing It,* the essay question was as follows?

'Write on a topic of your own choice related to the aims and learning outcomes of the module.'

What would help you choose something appropriate?

Read the module guide

In most cases the tutor will give some suggestions for topics to get students started and show the type of essay they are after. For this module the suggestions were:

- the presentation of a *problem, issue or theme* for contemporary children, such as the depiction of death, violence, family life, divorce, school, growing up, gender, class, race
- a particular *theoretical issue or debate*, such as the concept of bibliotherapy, censorship, the so-called 'new realism', the educational value of children's books, the ways in which books 'teach' (didacticism and the children's book)
- a particular *type* (genre) of children's book, such as the animal story, the futuristic novel, science fiction, fantasy, comedy, historical novels and so on.

Note and take account of any particular requirements

For this module, for instance, the tutor stipulated:

'Your assignment should review and evaluate **specific examples** of children's books in depth.'

This means that they want to see that you can *apply theoretical concepts,* ideas and frameworks to actual examples of children's books. You must, therefore, carefully choose those children's books if you want to do well.

Reflect on the aims and learning outcomes

For this module the aims were:

1 To provide an introduction to a range of modern children's authors and examples of their work.
2 To consider the **potential value** of the different literary experiences being created for children.
3 To identify and explore **the competing criteria** by which modern children's fiction may be **evaluated**.

The learning outcomes were that, after following this unit of study, students should be able to:

1 Identify, select and **contrast** a range of books written for children.
2 **Critically evaluate** the **potential value** of selected books for children and young people.
3 Demonstrate awareness of **the criteria** by which children's fiction may be judged and identify **their own criteria and framework** for making judgments.

These also give you a strong steer as to how to focus your assignment. They emphasize issues about the value of literature. They also flag up that perspectives on, and judgments of, children's fiction are important. In addition, the learning outcomes also emphasize that these issues should be discussed in relation to specific texts.

Reflect on the assessment criteria

Although not always available, in this example these were:

Content

- Clearly stated purpose, identifying, selecting and analysing an appropriate range of books for children, rationalizing the choice.
- Feasible scope and focus.
- Sustained, thoroughly developed argument, based on high-level understanding.
- Evidence of close reading of primary texts and use of relevant ideas from secondary theoretical literature.
- Evidence of appreciation, insight and understanding of key relevant issues, ideas and theories relating to the course.
- Evidence of awareness of relevant debates and dilemmas that surround the production and evaluation of texts for an intended child audience.

Structure

- Logical order, with clear signposts to let the reader know where the ideas are going and why they are important.

Style and presentation

- Appropriate academic style, with accurate referencing following departmental conventions.
- Grammar, spelling, vocabulary appropriate to selected topic.

They set out the possibilities and limits for your choice of title and offer clues on how to go about writing the assignment. They emphasize the need to apply theory from the secondary reading to primary texts, for instance.

(Continued)

(Continued)

In effect, the module guide gives you part of the recipe for successful assignment writing.

Now compare the way in which two students approached this assignment.

Ways of approaching the assignment: Student 1

The first student decided to write '**An exploratory study of teenage problem fiction**'. This outlined the range of problems that can be tackled in modern children's fiction for teenagers, including drugs, sex, pregnancy, alcohol, homelessness, growing up and puberty, divorce and identity formation.

The student explained how lots of books were written for teenagers designed to tackle these issues and problems, and summarized the plots of several, including two Judy Blume titles, one novel on teenage pregnancy written in the 1960s, one book on bullying, one high fantasy and one book from the 1990s on teenage relationships.

The student found an article saying that the teenage years were stressful and children needed books that helped them cope with the stresses of adolescent life. The introduction to the assignment cited this article, and a range of very generalized secondary literature which said that teenage fiction was an important and growing genre with a long history.

Finally, the student compared and contrasted the chosen books' approaches by pointing out that some used fantasy and some used realism to help teenagers come to terms with the problems they often face.

Tutor comments for assignment 1

- The assignment covered too much material and was not sufficiently focused.
- There was little awareness of the relativity of the many 'problems' discussed.
- While there was evidence of some wider reading it was very general and the student was uncritical of authorities (accepting, rather than questioning, comments about whether books help children overcome problems).
- The student did not think critically about the implication that child readers receive and accept a single message from any given book.

To summarize, the student did not perceive issues around the critical reception of books, nor the qualitative differences between the books' approaches to the problems they raised. The student earned a low 2:2. While they were hardworking, they were insufficiently tuned in to the key concepts and debates of the module and were descriptive rather than critical and analytical.

Ways of approaching the assignment: Student 2

The second student took a very different approach.

'An exploration of the critical reception of the work of illustrator Roberto Innocenti: the challenges of illustrating the Holocaust for young readers.'

This focused on Roberto Innocenti's illustrations, predominantly in *Rose Blanche* (2003) but also in Vander See's *Erika's Story* (2003). The assignment cited an article in *The Times* that questioned the suitability of these books for young readers, arguing that they would be 'puzzled' by the works. The student argued that Innocenti's pictures encourage a reader's questions and that he seeks to broaden the reader's understanding through this process of individual discovery.

The student also addressed questions raised by the review regarding the morality of exposing children to the Holocaust and responded to this by presenting the dangers of assuming that a child has no knowledge of suffering, in addition arguing that the emotions (fear, prejudice, anger, isolation) are feelings contemporary children share and experience in their own lives.

The student also drew on theory, particularly in analysing how Innocenti seeks to inspire connections between the protagonists through the concept of 'bridging metaphors' (Davies, 2000), which, thinking laterally, she drew from reading about citizenship education (as opposed to children's literature criticism).

Tutor comments for assignment 2

- This assignment was tightly focused and showed a clear engagement with the texts.
- The student had thought critically about authorities and critiqued their take on the way that children understand and interpret texts.
- An engagement had been made with the ways in which children's literature is evaluated.
- The student had drawn on a range of critical literature, applying it well to the examples chosen.

The student earned a First, having tuned in to the module's concerns effectively.

Now let's turn to compare different aspects of these two essays to clarify how you can learn from them and produce a good, focused assignment.

Titles

The title is very important. It steers the reader, ensuring that they understand what the assignment is about from the start. The first title is too broad, while the second is tightly focused and descriptive of the subject.

(Continued)

63

(Continued)

Arguments

In the first assignment, the argument (student's line of reasoning) is 'problem books help children'. This is too simplistic, and doesn't take account of opposing theoretical perspectives – it sees 'problem literature' as straightforward and 'problems' as uncontested. The student has just 'put in' irrelevant secondary reading on the history of teenage literature, rather than using her reading to construct a case and make relevant points. It is all about gathering information, not analysis. It fails to acknowledge controversy, challenge and debate. In contrast, the second essay appreciates complexity, arguing that Innocenti's work, while it has been seen by critics as problematic in relation to a child audience, can also be seen as an important route into exploring historical events. Further, she argues that the critics reveal the limits of their perception of children's literature and children through their comments about the books. There is an appreciation of possible meanings, values and judgments about children's literature, and various constructions of childhood, embedded within the argument.

These skills are important to develop, not just because they get good marks, but also because professional life increasingly values people who can compare different viewpoints. Multi-agency working requires professionals who can tune into different agendas and priorities. The capacity to argue why one approach is preferable to another, based on reason and evidence, is a strong leadership quality that is highly prized in childhood settings.

Mapping out and planning your ideas

When the student drew the plan for the first essay it had 'Teenage problems tackled' at its centre. 'Theory' only occupied one offshoot box (and was very limited, at that). Any other offshoot boxes had the titles of primary texts in them. It was, bluntly, too broad, unfocused and woolly, and she never refined her original working title. In comparison, the second plan had 'Objections to depiction of Holocaust for children' in the centre (note that this was an *issue*, which helped to strengthen the essay). The student used this as a working title, refining it as she went along, until it got sharper and sharper. She made sure her sharpest was the one she submitted. Other offshoot boxes had theoretical perspectives in them on, firstly, images, then reader response and multivalent texts, irony and, finally, secondary literature from liberationist perspectives (children have a right to know and be informed *or* children already live in world of violence/experience) versus protectionist ones (children should be kept in innocence), views which related to literature about constructions of the child such as James and Prout (1997). Further, there were boxes about children's rights debates and on teaching about the Holocaust (such as the writing by Davies). Finally, there were boxes focusing on analysing children's books in terms of, for example, the use of ending, the image of the child, the depiction of 'evil' and the use to which it is put. These boxes all became key subheadings in her assignment.

Many students find that mapping out the main ideas and seeing, visually, how material fits together helps them to adapt their reading, organize and develop their ideas and plan a structure for their assignment. Nowadays software tools such as Cmap (http://cmap.ihmc.us/download/) can be used, free of charge, to help with concept mapping.

Use of reading

The first student shows a limited awareness of a (one-sided) literature. The second student shows a higher understanding due to their wider reading and awareness of issues and concepts. She has grasped that criteria for evaluation are problematical and contested (something which the learning outcomes refer to). The writing draws on a wide range of literatures and applies them appropriately.

Tackling other types of assignment

You are likely to be faced with a range of assessment strategies on your CS/ECS course. However, essay/assignment writing still tends to be the predominant form of assessment. There are many variations, but they all demand approaches to preparation similar to that for an essay. Dissertations are considered in Chapter 4, with visits, observations and placements, as these learning events are often what inspire their focus.

For all the following, the basic rule is to check that you 'know your tutor' and seek out the assessment criteria.

Portfolios are becoming a common form of assessment. It is tempting to accumulate quantity instead of quality, but don't just hurl a load of material in. Tutors will want to see 'evidence' of your achievement in relation to specific learning outcomes. It's sensible to place your evidence (a lesson plan, an extract from a research diary you kept during a child observation or placement, an example of children's drawings, an annotated bibliography of reading or whatever else you've done during the module) into appendices and cross-reference these to

a) a contents page (closely tied to the specified learning outcomes and/or assessment criteria)
b) a discussion which highlights what you have learned, and draws attention to the evidence that can be found in your appendices.

The important thing is to help the reader find their way around your portfolio, rather than making them wade through lots of material.

Annotated bibliographies are set to encourage you to précis and summarize a wide range of sources, and test your skills of the synthesis, comparison and contrast of theoretical perspectives. Make sure, then, that you *say something* and make points about the reading you conduct (you will often be asked to 'critically analyse' it), rather than simply report it. Draw out similarities, differences and key perspectives.

Exams can be of several kinds. If the paper is to be seen in advance, then prepare as you would for an essay, but then, basically, learn that essay before you go into the exam hall. If it is an unseen paper, then you should see what past papers are available (to get a sense of the kind of questions asked), read through the module guide, especially the assessment criteria, and set yourself to memorizing material on the subject. You have been reading around, and what you know from that reading will make your answers richer.

Remember that it isn't facts that are usually being sought, but an argument, just like the essay, which draws on your secondary reading and your grasp of the issues. It is too easy, in exams, to write down everything you know about a subject rather than be selective and really answer the questions. Take a little time, after you have turned the paper over, to make sure that you have interpreted the question correctly, unpacking it as you would an essay question, rather than rushing into writing.

You may be asked to do **presentations** on your own or as part of a team. Again, make sure you know what, precisely, you are to present on, and prepare accordingly. Many students slip into thinking that presentations 'simply' test their presentation skills – whether they speak clearly, make eye contact with the audience, invite questions, have good visual aids and handouts, use PowerPoint and IT effectively and so on. This is, indeed, one aspect of presentations, and might be the main reason a lecturer uses it, especially in the early stages of your course.

On the other hand, though, most of the marks might actually be awarded for content – the sorts of things demanded in assignment writing – so check the assessment criteria. A presentation on the subject 'Show awareness of the implications of adult perceptions of risk on children's outdoor play', for instance, is clearly interested in the substantive topic area and research, not presentation skills. As we emphasized above, your assignment can look great, but if it doesn't have a well-developed focus and argument then it won't do very well and the same is true of presentations.

Reflective commentaries are increasingly being set in order to encourage self- and peer-review skills – and to reward the vital key skills that you'll need to do well in your studies and when you graduate. Again, make sure you know what they're after, and don't assume that they're asking for personal, opinionated writing. Lecturers will be looking for theorized thoughts that show what you have learned.

to think about

What is the focus of my reflective commentary supposed to be?

You might be asked to evaluate your own learning progress as part of a portfolio of evidence in the initial stages of your course. You can't just write 'I got much better'. Instead look at what lecturers want you to get better in. Imagine that the learning outcomes and criteria ask you to 'Appreciate that competing images and ideologies of childhood exist'. In response you could include, as an appendix, your summaries of different secondary reading you have done. In your reflective commentary you could draw out the different perspectives, highlighting their similarities and differences in relation to the views of childhood.

Another example might be a reflective commentary focused on getting better at writing about childhood and using theory, like the writing tasks on social construction we showed you in the last chapter. You could include, as an appendix, an early stab you made at writing a response on the early stages of your course (as seen in Chapter 2). A good reflective commentary would look at the strengths and weaknesses of that piece of writing and would also suggest what you would do to improve in future. You could include a redrafted piece of writing as another appendix.

Sometimes you will be asked to apply your knowledge to **design, project or problem-based/enquiry-based activities** i.e. a 'real world' issue, challenge or problem. An example might be 'Design a drugs awareness programme for teenagers, and theorize your response'. If you're asked to theorize or draw upon literature, you should offer your outline, but also discuss possible alternatives, showing *how* and *why* you have designed the programme the way you have.

to think about

Group tasks: collaboration versus collusion

Increasingly students are being asked to work with peers, formally and informally, during their studies. As we have emphasized throughout, working in

(Continued)

(Continued)

groups can add significantly to your learning, enabling you to share ideas, gain new perspectives, stimulate your thinking, clarify your understanding via dialogue and develop your interpersonal skills. Peers are an invaluable source of feedback.

If your group work is assessed, try to share tasks fairly, brainstorming potential problems and planning strategies for dealing with any difficulties. There are some useful guides to improving your group work, such as Moon (2009).

The learning gains of working with a supportive group of other students should not be underestimated. As one student said

> *Definitely I think you need to have a close network ... I think it would be very difficult to go through university life on your own because you need somebody just to say, you know, you are heading in the right direction.*

There are, though, a few risks to watch out for. Generally speaking, and unless tutors say otherwise, any writing you submit should be in your own words. Discussing ideas, chatting about reading, and passing on useful articles to read are all productive ways of working together. In group projects you may officially be required to share data collection or design a project together. As with wider reading, though, always make your own notes about the discussions and write the final assignment yourself. Never copy and paste another students' words into your own assignment, as they might hand in the same text, and this will be spotted. This includes references, where mistakes easily creep in and copying stands out like a sore thumb! It is generally unwise to let another student have open access to your work, other than to chat about it, because if someone copies it, you, as well as they, might be viewed as responsible for a form of cheating called collusion. Take care, then, to log out from networked systems you've produced work on and don't leave pen-drives or print-outs lying around. Also politely but firmly refuse if anyone asks you to do their work for them.

And finally ... using tutor feedback

It's vital to use and reflect on lecturers' written feedback – but tutors can use strange language, so you need to know how to translate it and, even more importantly, how to apply it as advice for the next assignment, as it is often generic and so applicable to more than one piece of work. Don't think 'I've done that one now, forget it and move on' – learn from feedback.

to think about

What tutors mean

These examples offer 'plain English' interpretations of tutor comments and what students could do in response to particular feedback.

Tutor comment: 'Your essay is strong on personal opinion'.
What this actually means is: You must learn to qualify statements.
What you could do to improve might include:

- analysing what the essay is asking you to do from the start
- using quotations to illustrate points
- further reading around the literature to uncover the range of perspectives on the issue
- citation of other people's views on the issue
- using wider reading to locate and back up different perspectives
- analysis of other people's perspectives
- comparing and contrasting other people's perspectives in the literature
- helping your reader locate any literature they may be interested in reading.

Tutor comment: 'You must learn to reference correctly'.
What this actually means is: You are not following the Harvard System, either within the body of the essay and/or in the reference list at the end.
What you could do to improve might include:

- evidencing all statements with authoritative comments based on recognized academic literature
- being cautious about the authority of material you get from the Web
- using a guide to the Harvard referencing system.

This will help because:

- the reader of your essay can see where your ideas have come from
- it helps you avoid plagiarism.

Tutor comment: 'Your essay is difficult to follow'.
What this actually means is: The argument is disjointed, does not follow a logical sequence, jumps from important to unimportant points randomly. There is no direction to the essay and it may even contradict itself.

(Continued)

(Continued)

What you could do to improve might include:

- planning your essay
- structuring it in paragraphs
- using subheadings
- proof-reading
- thinking about what the title is asking you to do
- sticking to the point
- working out your argument/establishing a central thesis statement
- asking someone to read the essay, for spelling and grammatical errors.

It is also very important to understand feedback if you have to do resits – use it to help you prepare.

Peer- and self-review as a source of feedback

It is not just written tutor comments on your work that constitute feedback, but also a range of information, including comments from peers and self-reflection.

Talking to tutors and fellow students (both in your current year group and the years ahead) can help you to clarify your own ideas. The 'not knowing what I think till I hear what I say' phenomenon emphasizes the importance of rehearsing and trying out your ideas in oral presentations, study groups and with others, however informally. If your course offers a mentoring or buddying scheme, such as PASS, get involved, or set up your own study support group.

Here's a student talking about how imperative it is to get used to working with others.

I like working with other people, and although it's a bit funny other people seeing your work, I've got used to it. Getting to know people in the tutorials has meant you feel OK about saying: 'Oh, I did it this way. How did you do yours?' And then you get the opinions of the whole group, not just your own ideas. So that's got to be better than doing it on your own. And you learn from making mistakes.

The following student comment also highlights how valuable it is to share your ideas and get feedback on how others are approaching an assignment. This is not a case of copying, but of getting useful alternative strategies for tackling assignments. This student has learned the need to focus from peers and concrete examples, as well as from tutors.

One of my [core module] essays was on child development. At first I was doing it overall, and it was quite hard, trying to cover everything, and do it justice, because I'd done a plan of all the aspects, and I chose the main ones we'd covered all through the semester. After I went to the tutorial [where group members discussed their essay plans], though, I saw it'd make more sense to choose one specific area of development, and really go for that. Because looking at the development of preschool children is so vast. So listening to other people, not so much tutors, but people on my level, really helped.

So, the final advice of this chapter is to start early, manage your time effectively, and build incrementally in writing assignments of any kind. Further, ask if you are not sure about anything and seek feedback from different sources on your interpretation of what is expected. Finally, revisit your work and check you're on the right lines by running ideas past peers and lecturers.

4

Visits, Observations and Placements

chapter themes

This chapter will help you to tackle the fieldwork, placement or 'real world' experiences you will be offered as part of your course but which will take place off-campus. It prompts you to see how and why these are important learning experiences, and offers guidance about effective ways of approaching them.

Why study CS/ECS beyond the university?

Often CS/ECS courses will take you out into the 'real world', rather than confining your studies to university classrooms. In different modules or units you might, for instance, be asked to undertake child observations, keep research diaries or practise developing other research skills by gathering data. You could be required to conduct interviews, archival work or surveys, or to evaluate child-related spaces, such as classrooms or libraries. Your course may incorporate visits or field trips into children's centres, schools, nurseries or other relevant settings. Some courses will include extended optional or compulsory placement elements, in which you will have the chance to develop the knowledge, practical skills and competencies involved in working as a qualified Early Years practitioner. There may also be the possibility of participating in an optional 'Students into Schools' unit such as one offered by Newcastle University and Northumbria University – see http://www.northumbria.ac.uk/brochure/visit/el/sis/.

Further, most students on ECS/CS courses will be required to undertake some kind of final-year independent research project, dissertation, personal study or extended piece of work, in which they must apply what they have already learned to explore or investigate a topic in some depth. These studies are often linked to an area of interest that students develop in specific settings, enabling them to work closely with particular professions, gaining valuable insight into different ways of working in particular contexts. Sometimes they can be linked to practical work being undertaken in settings.

It's important, then, as with other teaching and learning activities, to make sure you are clear in your mind about the precise nature and purpose of such off-campus placement activities and how they can benefit you and your learning. As you will have already discovered from reading the previous chapters, this is a matter of thinking acutely about your lecturers' perspectives and how they introduce this type of study to you. However, be aware that you can also use off-campus activities to focus on areas of individual interest as you move through the course, with your explorations getting more complex and focused as your degree progresses. As everyone has different interests, your choices and activities may not mirror those of your immediate peers. It's important, then, to think carefully about your own situation, skills, competences and levels of 'practical' experience.

Evaluating your own needs

Individual students on CS/ECS courses will usually possess different levels of 'hands on' experience. Thinking about the following issues means that you can really benefit from off-campus academic study.

 to think about

If you have come straight from school, you can see off-campus placement opportunities as a way to build up your knowledge of professional practice, enhancing your awareness of emerging themes, issues and challenges in relevant child-related settings. It will be useful to gain insight into the challenges of multi-professional working, for example, by observing this closely at first-hand.

(Continued)

(Continued)

If you are offered any choices regarding placements, or are required to establish your own, try and tailor these opportunities to your aspirations. For example, if you have a chance to choose the sorts of visits you make, or the research you undertake, you will want to ensure that you select wisely so that you build yourself a sound foundation for your intended professional future. If you are interested in going into teaching, for example, pick educational placements as real-world contexts for any study opportunities that take you beyond the university.

Extended placements can usefully help you to develop competence in working, say, as an Early Years practitioner in an accredited setting. However, as you will see in the next chapter, depending on the type of employment you hope to gain, you may also need to build up your 'hands-on' experience of working with children beyond the parameters of the course, so that you can demonstrate particular skills in applications for posts or interviews.

Be aware that this other 'work experience' often needs to be done in addition to some of the sorts of study opportunities we are outlining in this chapter, especially if extended placements are not offered within the course itself. Your university Careers Service will have information about volunteering and will support you in that role, – see, for example http://www.northumbria.ac.uk/sd/central/stud_serv/careers/students/comvol/. Search your university website using the term 'volunteering' to find out what opportunities are available to you. Remember that this can be a short term activity lasting just a few hours, or a longer term commitment, depending on what time you have available.

If you are already an established practitioner working with children in some capacity, your needs are likely to be rather different. You may be extremely familiar with your own setting. In this case you will benefit most from gaining some critical distance on that space. One course we are aware of for established practitioners offers the students the possibility of visiting and analysing each others' professional spaces and using that analysis as the basis of class discussion. Whilst such opportunities are rare, trying to develop a critical, yet positive, eye regarding your own setting and those of others is of great benefit professionally and means that you can act as a useful 'critical friend' to others, pick up good ideas and develop your habit of reflection on practice.

You might do this by setting yourself the task of exploring other ways of approaching practice-related issues, by making visits to alternative settings, shadowing, or investigating the views of a range of professionals. One of the authors of this book, who worked for many years as a children's librarian, is so embedded in the practice of visiting other settings that even when on holiday she informally seeks out children's libraries to see what the practice and space are like!

It is not uncommon on ECS/CS courses for work-based students to employ practitioner action research to improve their own professional practice or help move something forward in their setting, typically an innovation designed to support staff or children. In this instance it's important to think carefully about your identity as a learner and student, as opposed to your purely professional role, so that you make the most of opportunities to engage with issues on an academic as well as a practical level. In such circumstances, use the academic reading you have done as a way of helping you gain critical distance on practice or policy, contextualizing it within a broader understanding of, for instance, changes in education. Your student role can help distance you, in a good way, from the busy daily schedule of a setting and so help you get an overview.

Practical issues to consider

Learning in placements, and even making short visits to settings, will present you with challenging issues to think through and deal with. These will be focused on both academic work and on very practical issues about your role as student researcher. The following offers some advice about how to think about your placement or visit.

Remember you are a guest

Going on placement or making a visit is like going into someone's house for the first time. You wouldn't criticize their taste in decor to their face (or if you did, you wouldn't get asked back). It's the same whilst on a placement: you need to remember that you are not there to make anyone feel upset or uncomfortable. Familiarize yourself with their routines. Try to be open and sensitive to different professional boundaries. As you would if visiting a new friend's house, try to look out for the unspoken rules, like which seat 'belongs' to whom, which cups or rooms are OK to use, and offer to help out with any chores. Try not to take it personally, though, if people in the setting don't appear to be very welcoming: they may be busy, or feeling a bit nervous about having an outsider there, as you are a stranger to them and your brief is to observe. Think about how nervous you can feel when being watched doing an activity, like a presentation, for instance. They may feel a bit like that.

Remember that you need to observe the settings and practices you visit and think about them, but do not intervene or act unless invited to do so formally by those in charge in the setting, after that has been cleared with your university. We discuss this further below.

Be clear about your responsibilities

Your university should give you advice and guidelines about the norms, responsibilities and expectations of the setting, so that you understand them at the outset of any significant work-based or placement learning opportunity. Your course will also emphasize the importance of maintaining a safe environment. Further, your teachers should make clear what is expected of you in terms of behaviour and learning, and will cover important aspects such as the need for confidentiality, anonymity, safeguarding and child protection. These are important issues, so make sure you attend the relevant briefing sessions. Follow any guidelines you are given to the letter and ask your tutor if you are unsure.

When you are there, ask what you should do when practical situations occur, such as whether you should answer the telephone or open the door, so that you are clear about what to do. Make sure you also know what to do in an emergency. Become familiar with the setting's policy, such as what procedure should be followed if a fire occurs, and also what their first aid and accident procedures are. If you are concerned about a child's well-being, be clear about who you should inform and make sure you do so.

Not everyone in the setting may know who you are and why you're there, so be prepared to explain your role. Try to make clear, in advance, what it is you need to do for the course, so that it can be included in any scheduling, but remember that, as a guest, you can't make demands. If you are required to undertake specific tasks and feel out of your depth, ask, politely, if you may have more help, advice or support from the staff.

Your role as a student researcher

Remember, when you are in a setting in connection with your course, you represent the university, so behave professionally. Your actions will reflect on others, such as tutors and any future students who may need placements there. Of course you will need to be appropriately dressed, punctual and reliable, but this also means abiding by their rules, even if you don't fully agree with the underpinning philosophy. It is often very enlightening having a placement in a setting where you don't share the philosophy, as it can help you clarify, or modify, what you think and makes you aware of your own values, attitudes and assumptions. Find out what the rules are and then go with the flow of the space you are in.

If you are an established practitioner, or have chosen to explore a setting with which you are extremely familiar, other types of challenge could present themselves. Be aware that the 'rules' may shift or alter in your student role, necessitating that you change 'hats' from established practitioner to student very consciously.

In a familiar setting being clear with yourself and others about when you are there as student, and when you are there in your capacity as practitioner, will help. As mentioned above, whilst, as a practitioner your role may be to intervene, as a student that is very unlikely. You, and the setting, both need to know when you are in either role.

Similarly, if you are an established practitioner who is going into another setting as a student, it is important to leave your practitioner identity at 'home', as it is through your student/visitor identity that this setting will know you.

Being critical on placements

Think carefully about the values and personal views you have been learning about. You might find that you are more politicized than you think, and have developed strong views from your course about what is and isn't good for children. You might personally disagree with what you see of some educational practices or ways of interacting with, say, parents but remember, in your role as a researcher, it's not your place to comment, or pick holes in other people's work, as we discuss above.

This can be very tricky, of course, especially if it's a space you know well, but that just means you have to be doubly on guard. Your role as a researcher is not to criticize, in the sense of letting people know you disapprove. Nor are you there to try and change the world by forcefully imposing your opinions on others. Going in to 'prove' something is inappropriate, as is going in to tell people how you think they should do something.

Remember that as a researcher, the main thing that is likely to change is *you*, and this means keeping an open-mind, being reflexive, remaining aware of your own biases and sensitive to how your presence affects the data and your interpretations. You're there to learn, so achieve an *academic* level of critical enquiry, instead, by asking yourself questions, such as

- How do different members of staff deal with x (issue, practice or policy) here and what do I feel about that?
- How do I perceive this space?
- What do I think about x?
- Why might x be going on and what effect might it have on y?
- What are the obstacles to change when a setting tries to introduce a policy and what features appear to smooth the way?

Write your thoughts down in a learning/research log, so that you maintain a record of these and what inspired them.

If you are required to demonstrate competencies, use your learning log to reflect on how something you were required to perform went, and how you could try and improve it next time. Picking key critical incidents to talk about in detail is often useful in later assignments, so make sure you maintain sufficiently detailed notes.

to think about

- Do make sure that you keep any research notes private and secure.
- Don't publicly express a view.
- Don't get drawn into local politics. If someone stops you in the corridor to grumble about someone else, stay tactfully noncommittal.

If anyone, as an individual or a team, informally asks you for an opinion, remain neutral, even if they ask you to provide them with an 'expert' or outsider view. If you are asked formally to offer some sort of a report of your findings or a presentation to the staff, check with the university before you agree. As we mentioned above, this is vital. Remember, your course will make you officially aware if you should be having an impact in your setting. For example, if you are on a course where you are engaging in practitioner action research or work-based learning you will be carefully and explicitly guided through this process and will receive lots of appropriate support. If not, you should not seek to influence staff in settings.

Keep a focus on your student identity: think like a researcher

Whilst different students' personal circumstances and experiences of practice issues will vary immensely, everyone's aim should still be to *learn* from off-campus placements or fieldwork activities. This is where all the advice we offered in earlier chapters comes to the fore: when you are encouraged by your lecturers to go out beyond the university classroom, you need to think of yourself as someone who is, first and foremost, there to **learn, explore** and **investigate**.

Just as we suggested that you need to see yourself as a sense-maker, who actively tunes into other people's understandings and theories when you are reading, the same principles apply when studying in real-life settings. Your course will encourage you to do this by 'looking' at the real world through the theoretical lenses it promotes to you. When they send you out, or even if you are already in practice, lecturers will usually want you to get beneath the surface of whatever you are being asked to focus upon. Here is where you can put your critical, analytical skills to good use, by 'reading', interpreting and actively questioning the different stakeholder viewpoints and cultural practices you encounter in everyday child-related settings.

Throughout the earlier chapters we repeatedly emphasized the importance of understanding different theoretical positions and viewpoints, so that you could 'see' the host of complex and interrelated issues which surround childhood and can think critically, moving beyond taken for granted assumptions, popular myths and commonsense understandings. In an important sense this critical, questioning habit of mind is your foundation for thinking like a researcher, because you can use it to reflect on everyday experience. A researcher, after all, is basically someone who asks questions, analyses information and tries to illuminate something and aims to understand complex issues. If you think about it like this, research is a form of learning. The fact that it's taking place in real-life settings simply means you can practise developing your critical understanding in a real context, by linking theory to practice issues.

Beginning to link theory and practice

A real world dimension to your studies brings things to life and helps you see the point of the critical, analytical perspectives we covered earlier in the book. Indeed, often students will say it's going out into the real world that helps them see the point of all the reading they have done. This is a matter of actively making connections between theory and practice. One of our graduates offered the following advice:

> Let's face it, you don't want to sit for hours listening to theories that you can just read about in a book. You want to know how to do it! In order for you to experience theory in practice, it is essential that you create as many opportunities as you can to engage in meaningful ways with children in a range of settings. The only way to do this is to 'have a go' and get stuck in. It is your responsibility to make connections between what you hear, read and see and what you go out and do!

Once you recognize the complexity of childhood it naturally leads to asking questions, often a lot of them. There is always more to be learned about children, the people who work with and for them, and their different contexts. The sort of research that focuses on practical situations can help us view things about children and practitioners in new and different ways. By questioning habitual patterns of thinking we might arrive at suggestions for alternative ways forward. In other words, fuller understandings about what really goes on 'on the ground' can lead to future change. That's why, for instance, early childhood practitioners are being increasingly urged to become part of an 'evidence-based profession' which can adopt an informed, critical and open-minded position rather than simply managing various government policies.

Developing a critical stance, in the academic sense of the word, is key here. It means always asking questions about assumptions and beliefs, being aware of issues of power, and remaining continuously open to alternative viewpoints. These are all skills and qualities your course will foster throughout and are the hallmark of a graduate. Success, though, relies, as ever, on reading and grappling with academic perspectives: because it offers you particular viewpoints and issues to think about. If, then, you go into settings on your course, it is usually to learn – to act like a researcher – in this very specific way.

How do you know, though, what you should be learning while out on placement? Consider the following case study, which focuses on the in-class discussions that emerged from a visit to two early years settings. We'll present the visit itself in photos, so that you can see what we're talking about, and hear the sorts of questions the lecturer wanted her students to think about. These questions offer you a model of asking yourself questions, an important key to successful study. Once more, this is a process you'll develop through engaging in the sessions and activities lecturers make available.

 case study

Comparing and contrasting images of the child in school

An ECS lecturer on a module entitled 'Care & Education in Context' wanted her students to think about the implications of professionals' perspectives on childhood by getting them to consider how far different views of the child impacted on the services made available for the very young. This is a key issue in partnership working, which she wanted students to begin to appreciate.

First she asked her students to describe what they saw in two different settings in which children aged between 3 and 6 received care and education. She asked them to bring written responses to each photograph (Figure 4.1), which was of the entrance halls of the schools concerned. You can see the instructions and trigger questions she asked, together with one student's responses, below.

Figure 4.1   Images of early years settings

(Continued)

(Continued)

Describe what you see in both pictures

Picture A: Children have drawn their own pictures of themselves. They have written their own names. The pegs have their own bags and coats on them, all of which are different. It looks disordered and colourful. There's a collage above on the wall done by children.

Picture B: Each name sticker is on a very symmetrical peg. Every sticker has been done professionally on card, they are all the same size and have a glossy image of an animal. Adults have written the child's full name on each. The pegs have got the children's coats on. Some bags are different, but most are peg bags made identically in the same material as used for uniforms. It looks quite orderly. There are certificates on the wall.

How are they the same?

Both identify the children and name them as individuals. They are the space where children bring and leave their own possessions. They both seem to be in the entrance hall. Both have adult versions of writing.

How are they different?

The first one children have drawn and labelled their own space, and have done a representation of themselves to identify this. Emphasis on drawing rather than writing. They recognize through a picture they have drawn. The second one is not a picture of their own making. The first one has a jumble of different items, whereas the second one has a very similar set of items, that all look like school possessions. The first one offers the child a chance to develop their own space. But the second one is done by the adult.

What do you think adults in each setting would say are the reasons why they have developed their particular entrance area the way they have?

In the first one they want to encourage the children to bring what they have to the school, to feel a sense of belonging and be part of the school and to recognize their difference. To welcome diversity and recognize that you are an individual.

In the second the setting is saying this is how we do things here. These are the routines that help children to become part of this school. This is levelling the children, protecting them from difference and sharing the school identity and community.

What do you think the adults in each setting feel is important for children's learning?

In the first setting they value children learning about themselves as individuals, how they are different from each other, taking some measure of control of their space and environment, learning to value and recognize difference. They want them to practise emergent writing, but it's OK to have a go, even if it doesn't look perfect.

The second setting values conformity to the expectations of others, to learn that they are not special or unique, to view adults as models and to meet adults' expectations in school, to achieve high standards by learning from best examples, to follow an expert, that there is only one way that is right that you should strive to reach.

You can see how the lecturer's trigger questions have guided the student to move beyond simple description by encouraging her to analyse rather than simply 'look'. By consciously setting out to compare and contrast different perspectives on childhood, the student has begun to identify the critical issues that begin to emerge. There is no suggestion from lecturer or student that either is 'wrong', just that they contrast and reveal different ideologies about the role of education. This links back to what we mentioned about going in to settings to observe, not to judge or try to impose your own values on staff or the setting.

Learning to ask yourself questions about why things are as they are, or why people hold certain values, or why policies don't smoothly translate into practice, or how people construct and reveal views of children's needs is essential to thinking like a researcher who links theory to practice. If you have got into the habit of using sessions to tap in to the relevant issues, identifying the 'big questions' and rehearsing your responses to different ways of addressing them, you should be well placed to successfully approach any placement with an enquiring, open, but informed mind.

The following student, who was already an established practitioner in an early years environment, remembers how her appreciation of theory in her first year started to spark questions in her mind about her own workplace.

It really, really made you think and it really made you challenge some of the things that you saw and think about well, why is it done like that? For whose benefit is it? And I really do question things more, and I start to think more about early years education for children. Just for whose benefit is it that we are pushing these young children in their cognitive development and not really thinking as much that their emotional social is as important? And it does make you think there's a bigger picture here and maybe the children are sort of manipulated along the way and given very little choice.

Whilst these are very general questions, by the end of the first year she was well-placed to look out for specific issues of interest on which to focus her enquiry in later years.

Developing your research skills

Often courses will incorporate child observations into your studies, some-times from quite early on. Let's think about why that might be the case. Researchers will take account of different ways of seeing, but they will do so in a systematic way, so your course may seek to develop specific research skills that will help you look and analyse on an appropriate level and in a methodical way.

 to think about

Why do child observations?

Courses commonly offer practical hands-on work to anchor your understanding of child development, so you may observe young children at first hand. This is not like the sort of checklist approach you might be used to from previous courses. Instead, it aims to look beneath the surface, suspending your assumptions, watching and listening in an active way, and becoming open to why things might happen in a surprising way. This is 'seeing' in a new way, so that what might appear as familiar, everyday behaviour is made distant and strange.

Look for different points of view

Looking critically does not mean pulling something to pieces, but thinking about it in the light of your reading on the topic and asking yourself why it might be that people are behaving in the ways they are. Being aware of different points of view is central and thinking about different possibilities might open up and change your understanding of the topic, as we have mentioned before.

So on placements try to form a sense of different people's preoccupations, values, attitudes and opinions by listening to what they say and watching what they do. You will often find that critical issues you have studied reveal themselves as live debates in real world situations and prompt lines of enquiry you may wish to pursue in your final year research project.

case study

Looking out for critical issues

For instance, a student who had been studying issues surrounding children's literacy development remembers witnessing an incident in her local library which made her notice the ways in which some of the debates we'd been having in class were played out in real life.

> *The other day I was in the library when a child wandered from the children's section into the adults' section. That met with different reactions, I can tell you! One man was tutting at the mother and going 'You can't go bringing her into the adult section. Making a noise and a nuisance!' And her mother was 'Well, how is she going to learn to read as an adult if she's not allowed to get hold of the books?' Seeing this happen in real life, it sort of put it into a real context and I could relate to it.*

In a class discussion back at the university, she remembered how her tutor encouraged her to view this as a critical incident which was worth studying more closely. The lecturer seemed pleased to discuss it because it had showed the student, in a forceful manner, how different people interpreted the child's act in very different ways. Once the incident had sparked the student's interest, she began to wonder about what might count as 'good practice' for all of these people. In other words, she was now in a position to look for a range of perspectives within the literature on children's reading. Gradually, stemming from this one incident, she decided to focus her final year study on a systematic investigation into various perspectives on children's use of the library, focusing on gathering and analysing a spectrum of individual librarian's views.

Looking for hidden agendas

Sometimes, though, people's agendas will be more hidden, and carried beneath the surface. You can tune into these agendas by listening out for the varied words that are used by professions, individuals or disciplines. This is especially important at a time when multi-agency working is seen as the key to safeguarding children, as those working in different professions will often use very varied terminology to discuss the same thing. They may also use a word that is used in other professions, but it may carry a different meaning! Studying like this gives you the chance to gain deep insights into different stakeholders' perceptions and interpretations, raising your awareness of the mismatches that can occur between people's views. Further, learning to listen out for tensions and issues in relationships or contrasting outlooks is a vital skill in your ability to manage future professional changes and respond to challenging situations.

To this end, try to use your final year project productively, by following the pointers in the next chapter and learning to choose a useful focus for your real world investigations.

5

Doing your Dissertation or Research Project

chapter themes

- The chapter includes advice about undertaking your final year project, independent study or dissertation, which typically involves some form of real world research.

Producing a good dissertation

An independent project or dissertation is a typical assessment in the final year of any CS/ECS Honours degree. This usually involves collecting some 'real world' data, gathering information on the views, opinions and perspectives of stakeholders, such as parents, teachers, police, medics, children, librarians, health visitors, nursery officers, or exploring dimensions of practice, such as work with children in classrooms, retail, looked after children, social services, respite services, or youth services. You'll usually be expected to use research methods such as interviews, participant observation, research diaries or questionnaire surveys.

This may sound daunting, as do the words 'doing research'. Some people panic at this point and forget what they know about writing good assignments, which is a shame as doing a dissertation or project is very similar.

Finding a good research question

Remember that your research question might actually look like a statement. Try saying *'In my study I want to find out more about x. I want to look at this issue because ... '*. A research question is not usually something you can answer in a straightforward manner: it's more likely to be an *area* you explore or an *issue* to address. The word 'research', however, sometimes makes students see it as a strict scientific exercise, in which they try to prove something, even though the course has focused on illuminating different perspectives. In fact, ECS and CS courses are rarely about being wedded to one idea and setting out to prove it right. They aim, instead, to dig deep.

Try to see this as your chance to look deeply at something you have developed an interest in, and an opportunity to study something in the real world. You should know, by now, that you can do research by using books and journals. You should know that any theme or issue needs to be contextualized, by summarizing the different perspectives you will find in wider reading. You should know how to analyse and be critical. So don't get alarmed by doing your research project, it simply extends this a bit into a real setting. You can do it!

The size of the project, as it can typically be 9–12,000 words long, may also create panic and cause students to choose a topic that is simply too big. However, once students get into writing their dissertation they will always say it's far too *few* words to say what they want to say and their advice would be to *focus on a sharper topic*. You will have been doing shorter pieces of writing that follow the same rule for several years by this point, so don't be troubled by the larger scale.

In effect, what makes a good assignment also makes a good dissertation or project. General principles apply: just as you will need an 'angle' in your assignments, based on theoretical explorations of debates and issues, so you will need one for a dissertation. Moreover, a good project will, as in an essay, often start by looking for varying perspectives, and the reasons people hold those views, within the context of a general topic. As in shorter assignments, looking for varied perspectives and summarizing secondary reading are the main ports of call.

There are lots of books to help you with projects and research/dissertations, which you should refer to in detail, for example, Bell (2005), Levin (2005) and Roberts-Holmes (2005). In what follows, though, we offer a few pointers to help you avoid some classic mistakes and enable you to deal with some commonly held anxieties.

Choose an interesting topic

A dissertation enables you to have more choice and control, but needs high levels of personal commitment and self-management. So reflect on what personally and professionally interests you, as then it will maintain your interest and allow your enthusiasm to shine through. Often you will find that the research interests of some very experienced researchers started from a personal incident, or something that happened to them. Make sure you choose something that will really make you tick, as this work could well be underpinned by principles and values which will occupy you for a long while after your degree!

 case study

Choose a topic you're interested in

As an undergraduate Mary was interested in disability studies and her child-centred values meant she became passionate about researching children's voices. In her dissertation she explored children's views of inclusion in curriculum decision-making. Because she respected children's abilities, she was committed to trying a variety of methods to listen to their voices and facilitate their participation. Mary's research interests developed further during her professional life as an early years educator and have, 11 years later, become a basis for her PhD and a university lectureship.

Choose something with limited ethical considerations

It's important to focus your work in such a way as to minimize ethical concerns. Ethics are much more complex than designing a tick-box form which offers your participants confidentiality. Instead, they should inform everything you do, including the development of your research question. This is one reason why it's important to share your ideas with your supervisor, sooner rather than later, as the following case study highlights.

case study

Developing your research question

As she started her final year, Carly didn't have a clue what to do for her dissertation. Because she was required to produce an outline plan by the end of the first month, she panicked. She remembered being interested in a session on girls' perceptions of body image in her second year, so did a quick online search and found a lot of articles claiming that the media were causing problems for teenage girls. She took her proposed title – 'How does the media effect girls' body image?' – to her supervisor, together with a list of the articles. She planned to interview teenage girls about their body image and show how far the media had influenced them.

The supervisor was concerned about the title and asked Carly to think about how far she thought it was possible to measure these 'effects' and answer the question she had posed. He asked if Carly had looked for any literature which offered alternative perspectives. He wondered to what extent the articles Carly had found might relate to anxiety accounts of supposed 'media effects' debates, and how they might reveal the attitudes of the researchers, who saw children as socially incompetent in a negative, or at least 'blank slate', model of childhood. He also asked if any literature suggested that different girls might see things differently.

Carly discovered, then, that her information search had been too narrow. The search terms she had used had meant that she had only located studies which viewed the media as a problem and cast the child as their victim, and she hadn't looked for material which questioned this cause and effect interpretation and saw the child as potentially powerful and competent and which respected children's abilities. Nor had she considered theories of gender, which had been covered on the course. In other words, Carly had not read widely enough in her chosen topic and had also not thought laterally about the relevance of themes raised throughout the course. Her supervisor was concerned that she hadn't acknowledged the different ways in which the issue could be understood from a theoretical viewpoint, including views of the child as a competent social actor.

The tutor also wanted Carly to think about how aspects of her intended line of questioning might lead to upsetting her participants. Carly was planning to touch on sensitive issues and ask intrusive questions, which might make children think there was a problem with them or their behaviour. The tutor reminded Carly that it was the researcher's responsibility to minimize the risk of posing emotionally upsetting and intrusive questions and asked her to reconsider her focus.

At first Carly felt devastated, because she was being advised not to undertake the project as it stood. She felt that her ideas were being rejected and she was being prevented from what she wanted to do. Once she talked to her classmates, though, she began to see that actually she was being asked to refine rather than reject her ideas. She found that other students had panicked, too. Someone had said the research project had to be original, so students had chosen 'new' areas to explore, because they were frightened of handing in work that had already been covered. When they asked the module leader about this, however, she explained that in this circumstance 'originality' might simply mean doing a study with a new group of people/in a new context, rather than starting entirely from scratch.

Carly looked up her notes from all the modules she had covered and asked herself what issues might be relevant to her project. She found she had a lot of useful theoretical material already. Gradually, Carly refocused her project to explore different adults' views of magazines marketed for teenage girls and, working with her supervisor, produced a good piece of work which extended some of the material she had already covered and reworked it in a particular context. In the end, she set out to illuminate a range of outlooks on the issue, rather than looking to 'prove' only one.

You need to reflect continuously on the ethical dimensions of your project and any placement activity. Asking yourself the following questions will help.

 to think about

What potentially sensitive issues am I asking people to talk about?
How could my questions be taken the wrong way?
How might I leave participants worried or cross in any way?
If it were me (or children I know well), would I agree to (let them) become part of this research?
How might my questions have a negative impact on the setting?
Could my research upset any relationships or open up the setting to disapproval?
What advantages might there be from people getting involved in this research?

If your supervisor is concerned about any of the above, they will advise you to rethink your research questions. If supervisors tell you they are concerned, don't take it hard, but think about *why* they are worried. They don't want to stop you because they're mean, or because you're wrong, but will help you reframe your research so as to minimize the risk. They might suggest, for instance, that you seek professionals' views, rather than children's.

Working with your supervisor

As we have seen, choosing a sensible topic is vital. So don't put it off and seek your supervisor's advice earlier rather than later. You will need to work in partnership, so try to strike up an efficient working relationship with them. Supervisors will have an excellent sense of what will work in a final year project, because they see so many, but they can only give you feedback if you go along to meetings prepared to talk about your interests. Waiting to be told what to do next won't help. Run your ideas past them, however silly you fear they might be: these will form a starting point. Keep a log of your meetings as well. It's useful to remind yourself what you discussed and it also helps you see and discuss your progress. Together you can agree sensible actions and timescales, and this can guide your next meeting.

Refine and change your ideas as you go along

As we have seen, the key to success is developing a good research question. Build in time for this because it can take a while, as can be seen in the next case study.

 case study

A student became interested in the issue of how few men there seemed to be in the childcare settings she'd visited. She knew this was a topical issue, and that there was debate about how difficult it was to attract men to childcare roles, and, further, that opinion was divided about whether it was deemed 'a good thing' to recruit men to work in nurseries. On the one hand, men could be seen as positive role models for children by, for instance, challenging stereotypes of men as uncaring, but on the other hand, she knew male carers met with resistance and suspicion.

This was still, however, too big a focus. One way to narrow down her project was to think about whose views she might want to research. She could have looked at employers' perspectives on the challenges and issues surrounding men in childcare, or she could have looked at parents' perspectives, or other (female) nursery officers' views.

This student chose, however, to explore the views of male nursery officers themselves. She identified and interviewed male nursery officers in her region and compared and contrasted their views about being in this role, about other people's perceptions of them, about what drew them to the profession, about barriers and rewards – in sum, how they felt about themselves in relation to their professional identity as men in a female-dominated profession. This meant her project started to focus on questions of personal identity and she became immersed in the literature on identity and construction of self.

Depending on the research question she could also have taken the literature search in other directions, for example into literature on masculinities, or on managing people. In effect, there is no 'correct' literature, just a huge range of potential sources of ideas and concepts.

 case study

Choose a topic to help your intended career

Cate wanted to teach and specialize in English. She decided, therefore, that she wanted to focus on the National Literacy Strategy for her dissertation.

Again, she had to focus down, and decided to concentrate on the issue of shared reading. Her inspiration was observing teachers deliver the literacy hour and noticing the differences in their use of shared reading. Her initial survey of the literature revealed different perspectives on the value and purpose of reading – from Cooling (1998) and Dombey (2000) who valued imagination, promotion and a whole-book approach, to a very different view based around skills development.

Cate had also noticed that not all teachers used story-time, and decided to see, when they did, how their views of its value compared and contrasted. Her dissertation became about teachers' views of delivering literacy via shared reading and she interviewed two experienced and two newly qualified teachers as part of her research.

Let's look at Cate's progress in more detail, to illuminate some other related areas of doing well in dissertations.

Reporting the data you collect effectively

Most dissertation assessment criteria (and, incidentally, any other more 'practical' or research-led reports or fieldwork-based assignments you might be required to do on CS/ECS courses) will focus on your data analysis skills.

Cate eventually reported her findings under subheadings, which she established by looking for key themes and issues in the interview data.

The subheadings she used were:

1 *Teachers' concerns about the National Literacy Strategy.* All four teachers mentioned the fast pace of the National Literacy Strategy and expressed concerns about differentiating the curriculum for children with special educational needs. However, there were marked differences, which formed the basis for the next subheadings.

2 *Teachers' views of the value of the National Literacy Strategy.* Experienced teachers were annoyed by this and found it intrusive and prescriptive. Newly qualified teachers expressed no concerns. Cate backed up this general point by quoting a teacher as an illustration: 'The children keep stopping to focus on capital letters and full stops: they'll even shout out every time they see a capital letter! But reading should be enjoyable, not reduced to being treated like a quiz or a puzzle'.

3 *Teachers' views of the autonomous learner.* The student noted marked differences in the levels of responsibility teachers expected or demanded of the children. She talked about how often experienced teachers used words like 'independently' and encouraged the children to 'join in'. New teachers, by contrast, seemed to have a view of passive children: 'I like the children to sit on the carpet and for me to teach the skills. I can keep track of the objectives I'm teaching this way'.

4 *Motivation.* Experienced teachers believed children were motivated by reading whole books, making comments like 'Story-time is good because it opens up discussion' (using the term 'opens up' also suggests this teacher valued children having a say or an opinion). These teachers also valued fun: 'I love to see the excitement on their faces during story-time.'

New teachers, in comparison, used reward systems to motivate – giving out stickers and stamps for 'working hard': 'I don't stop and discuss the pictures. One main reason for having story-time is to help develop their listening skills, as they have really bad listening skills.'

Instead of simply reporting what the teachers said, Cate concentrated on making points about the teachers' views. For example, she wrote

One possible interpretation is that because the newly qualified teachers appeared to view the learner in a passive role, they then felt that it was their duty to be teaching the learner some sort of skill. During story-time it is listening skills.

It is important to note that key themes are not 'fixed'. They depend on your 'angle', your research question and the design of the research instruments (the ways of collecting data, devising interview schedules and so on) and your awareness and 'take' on the reading you have done.

So, then, how did Cate pull out these themes and produce such a good dissertation? First she chose a *research question* that looked for different perspectives, based on contrasting stakeholders' views, and she explored how these views compared to the theories (perceptions of value) she'd read about. She used her literature review to set the scene for the reader, by identifying and summarizing the varying viewpoints, arguments and debates, which she got from her background reading as a context for her study. She showed that she had read widely and could weave together the arguments from different areas into a coherent whole.

When she came to gather and subsequently report on her data, she collected and analysed these systematically, informed by her reading and understanding of the topic area. This gave her key headings to work with. She produced these by a process of:

(a) summarizing each interviewee's viewpoint (known as data reduction) – précising their views by condensing them onto separate sheets of paper (one per teacher).
(b) comparing and contrasting the sheets of paper, deliberately looking for similarities and differences between the teachers' views. To do this she picked out the main themes and issues, then set about coding everything each teacher said by asking key questions of the data:

 – trying to assess the strength of support for particular views
 – looking for opinions for or against
 – looking for any gaps or surprising omissions (things they might have been expected to say), which implies she had read around the issues before starting her research.

This process allowed her to go through all the interview transcripts (raw data) in a systematic way, coding bits of text by using different coloured highlighter pens. This then gave her a framework for discussing her findings. These were in turn related to the literature review chapter, and she had identified illustrative quotes from the interviewees to include as evidence in her report, as we discussed above.

Data analysis and coding

The following example shows what we mean by this in a little more detail. Here are a number of extracts from interviews with different parents about their views of the purposes of outdoor play.

 case study

Parents' views of outdoor play

1

I don't know, I mean, you hear so much about kids having accidents when they play out. They're bad enough when you've got them with you; I know our Carl's always hurting hisself even when he's just in the garden at home. And that's when there's just him and me with him all the time. So, well, I don't know, I like to think he's in the house and I know where he is.

2

Well, my lot just love being outdoors. They come in filthy mind you, but, well, you can't really enjoy yourself and not get mucky when you're that age, can you? I remember when me and Pete, my brother, we used to nip off down the rec, like a big park with woods and that near our place, and we used to get up to all sorts. Course, nowadays you'd be worried for strangers and perverts, but then we used to just play and build dens and make up stories and it was our special place. No grown ups. Just us. That's what we liked, being able to do our own thing and no one telling us not to.

3

You mean, if they were at nursery and they were just playing out all day? I'm not sure about that at all. I mean, what do you send them to school for if they're just doing stuff they could do at home anyway? I mean, they've got time enough to play out on the weekends and heaven knows. They've got precious little time to learn all the stuff they need to get through before they're getting sorted into sets for Maths and sets for English. And my two, well, it's hard enough to get them to sit down and concentrate on anything for more than 30 seconds as it is. They'd like nothing better than to be up and out rolling in the mud all day and building dens and the like. But that's not going to be much good to them when they leave school is it? You don't see many jobs with 'hut building' in them! No, if Mrs T at the nursery started on that lark I'd be thinking about moving my boys.

4

For me, it's about giving them a chance to have a bit of freedom for once. Kids nowadays, they seem to be always being bombarded by what they're meant to be doing, not what they want to do. I don't agree with that. It puts pressure on parents to hear their reading. It's like you're a bad mother if you just have a romp. Last Sunday we all went down to the Dene and hunted for conkers. I used to love that when I was a kid. And Terry, he was really good at it. He kept thinking of ways to get them down, out of the trees and he made up this game where he was a squirrel and we all had to chase him and try and find his secret hoard. And at the end, I don't know, we just seemed to be closer, much closer than if we'd spent the morning doing homework or something. And on the way back we stopped off at his gran's and she dug out some pictures of me when I was his age and she reminded us of how me and our Lynne used to meet up with the kids along the way and built a bogey, you know, a cart sort of thing, and used to give each other rides. I'd forgotten till she reminded us, but it was really good. In fact, I've probably forgotten half the stuff I did when I was a kid, but that just brought back so many memories, you know: of being young and having fun, and secrets, and I suppose that's the kind of memories I want my kids to have. Not all school and studying and doing worksheets. More about having fun and feeling you're more ... not just always doing what your mum or your teacher tells you.

5

You worry though, don't you? I mean about what people will say about you if they see your kids outside, especially at night or if it's dark early. It's just there's so much nowadays about stranger danger – you can hardly open the paper without reading about some kid that's been abused. And we don't even know half the time that there's blokes with records for that sort of thing living in the area. As a parent you just can't be too careful. You've got to look after them. I'd never ever forgive myself if anything happened to any of my kids.

6

I suppose I'd be a bit worried about what they'd be getting up to. I mean, you know what they're like in the playground, that's when all the trouble seems to happen. And it might sound all very nice: freedom, exploring, playing and stuff, but my little girl, well she's quite nervous you know. And some of the lads in that nursery they can be quite naughty and rough and they're quite

(Continued)

(Continued)

> *a handful to the teacher even when they're in the class. So I'm not sure that I'd be certain my daughter would be really safe if they were running around all over the place and not being like closely supervised you know.*

For the first step (data reduction) you could briefly summarize each one's viewpoint, with a bullet point giving a brief overview of what each is saying about children playing outdoors. You could then move your analysis further by highlighting those 'for' and 'against': parents 2 and 4 are for outdoor play while 1, 3, 5 and 6 are against it.

Next, having looked at the data, think of possible categories/subheadings to report your work under. This helps you engage with the possible reasons why parents hold their views, and focuses you on the differences, as well as the similarities.

For	Against
Views of children's independence, autonomy and choice	Risk and adult protectionism (i.e. independence seen as threatening)
Skills development	Perceptions of time wasted
Children need freedom to explore	Children need protection/teaching by adults. Perceptions of risk
Good parents enable	Fears of being labelled a 'bad' parent
Romantic views of the child	Fears of children as violent or aggressive

These broad categories are not the end of the story, however, but can serve to get you started. Like Cate, you could use quotations from the data to show that the picture is more complex again, reading further into interviewees' perspectives – just like we said about reading into and analysing secondary texts. What's important is that you begin to see there's a lot to be said about your data, so that you focus down in a sharper way, if you need to. Too many students don't make the most of their research when it comes to writing it up, because they haven't sufficiently analysed it and included illustrative quotations.

For example, some parents shared a concern about a particular issue, but for different reasons. Both 6 and 5 offered comments that fall under the subheading 'Children need protection'. However, 6 is concerned about protecting her child from other children: ' ... I'm not sure that I'd be certain my daughter would be really safe if they [the lads] were running around all over the place and not being like closely supervized ...' In addition, in citing boys as the problem, she is flagging up gender issues around outdoor play. In contrast, parent 5 sees other adults as the issue: 'It's just there's so much nowadays about stranger danger – you can hardly open the paper without reading about some kid that's been abused', a very different view of what is ostensibly the same issue.

Similarly, you could imagine a subheading on views of the child. Views were often underpinned by varying notions about a 'proper' childhood. Some parents saw the child as inherently independent and appeared to subscribe to Romantic views of children. One, for example, held the view that outdoor play was a valuable way to share the family heritage and stimulate emotional development, saying: 'For me, it's about giving them a chance to have a bit of freedom for once'. Further, 4 argued that outdoor play 'brought back so many memories, you know: of being young and having fun, and secrets, and I suppose that's the kind of memories I want my kids to have'.

Another subheading or theme could surround views of adult roles and responsibilities. Here you could discuss interviewees' perceptions that were related to views of the role of parents as protectors/policing and ensuring safety. As 1 said, ' ... I like to think he's in the house and I know where he is'. Other points you could make when unpacking the data could relate to views of the role of adults as educators and the view that outdoor play is perceived as time wasting. As 3 argued, 'But that's not going to be much good to them when they leave school is it? You don't see many jobs with "hut building" in them!' Others seemed worried about being labelled as an irresponsible parent. As 5 said, 'I mean about what people will say about you if they see your kids outside, especially at night or if it's dark early'.

In your write-up, you would relate each theme to theoretical viewpoints expressed in the literature.

Edit your work

Don't see the production of your thesis as a linear, step-by-step thing, but as a recursive process. Continually go back over it, revisit and refine each aspect – your topic, methods, reading, evidence, analysis, writing up. You will need to be open to changes in direction and even to 'cutting' some really good bits. As one student put it:

> I once saw a telly programme about the man who made the film The Sixth Sense. He was saying how hard it was to cut some scenes he'd made, which he really liked. But cutting them was best for the overall effect of the film. Focusing can be like this: sometimes less is more.

Be aware, too, that reading is an ongoing process. Often what somebody said or did can lead you to reading and asking different, slightly refined research questions, so don't stay too fixed in your approach. Continually refine your literature review in the light of your findings.

Finally, when writing up, sort your material into categories and interweave it with your reading. Make sure you make points and say something about the data and reading you include, so your reader knows why you have chosen material. Your job is to sort it all out so the reader can follow your argument and see what you have learned and what it might mean. Don't make your reader do all the work and definitely don't just stick all your raw data in an appendix at the back, allowing this to speak for itself, unless you are officially advised to do so. Your role is to draw your reader's attention to aspects you wish to highlight. Besides, including raw data might compromise your assurances of anonymity and confidentiality.

Writing up your conclusions

Think about the implications that might be drawn and show how your findings relate to existing work in the area. You might be asked to include your reflections about what worked well and less effectively during the research process. This is not the place to talk about practical or personal issues, such as the batteries dying in your digital recorder, or the time constraints you faced because of work commitments. Nor is it the place to apologize for shortcomings, such as not having made time enough to pilot your questions. Instead, discuss, say, ways in which your status in the setting might have influenced the responses, or the ways in which your focus might have impacted on the data.

Placements, research and employability

Finally, try and enjoy your time studying off-campus. Doing research offers you invaluable experience and insight when it comes to life after your degree, as the next chapter highlights. Further, you will learn a lot of skills you will need as part of a graduate workforce, as this student observed:

> Now I can come in here (an early years setting) and analyse the space, think critically about it. No way could I have done that before.

This is far from easy, however, as the following student says, but do persevere, because it certainly develops the skills you will need when it comes to future employment:

> I think research is about learning how to find things out. Being critical and being able to analyse. It's hard at first, quite scary, then it gives you confidence. It gives you more confidence in yourself as a person because you feel you can put your point across more strongly, with reasons for your views.

6

Life Afterwards: Getting a Job and Further Study

chapter themes

This chapter will explore a range of directions that you might consider taking after leaving university. It is designed to help you benefit from the experiences of people who have finished CS/ECS degrees and have moved into the world of graduate employment.

Here, former students talk about the jobs and courses they are doing now and how their university studies are helping them to be successful. Sometimes you will hear them discuss things they did that helped them get ahead of the competition for jobs, or things they wish they'd done when they were undergraduates. Getting advice from those who are 'wearing the t-shirt' will help you see the sorts of things that you can do while you are still at university to improve your chances of preparing for, finding and getting future employment you will enjoy.

By listening to their stories you will pick up some useful ideas about:

- the sort of career and further study options that are available to you and what these various options might involve.
- the sorts of knowledge, skills and qualities that these careers and further study might involve and so where to start regarding applications and interviews.
- developing key skills, including critical thinking, which will stand you in good stead to apply for and pursue further professional qualifications.
- building up a personal profile of expertise and gaining relevant experience.
- using your degree to develop new interests and widen your horizons.
- adapting the course to suit your own individual needs and interests.

Where do I go from here?

Getting to grips with the university experience is challenging and exciting enough without thinking about graduating and starting a career. Whilst some people will have a specific career in mind when they begin their studies, most will use the time spent at university to explore possibilities, particularly through placements, if they are part of the degree. It is worth asking yourself the question, 'Where do I want to be in five years time?' from the very start of your studies and returning to it regularly. As you progress through the degree, reflecting on this question will help you adapt the course to your needs and desired career.

The key issues that your assignments focus upon are likely to be relevant to employers, as graduates state throughout this chapter, so these will come into their own in your life after university. For that reason, it's a good idea to make the most of assignments in which you are asked to discuss and explore them. The sooner you see their relevance, the sooner your studies will all fall into place, helping you to make the most of your time at university – even modules that don't seem directly connected to your chosen career.

You might also like to reflect on which modules you have enjoyed the most as you went through your degree, as they might point towards careers that you would like to enter. You may change your mind about where you want to go after graduation, given the range of possibilities that these subject areas can open up.

Keeping a learning log

Because courses vary so much, you will need to think about the ways in which your particular CS/ECS degree is valuable and relevant for the career you wish to pursue. This will mean you can market your course related skills and knowledge effectively.

Successful students often choose to draw employers' attention to the nature and value of the independent research skills that have been developed on their degrees and keeping records of that in a learning log can help. For example, if you are going into higher degree work, or contract-research, you will want to illuminate what you know and have learned about the research process. The following graduate, now working as a research assistant, looks back and reflects upon the way in which she could perhaps have sold her skills and qualities more forcefully and confidently, had she realized them at the time she applied for research posts.

I'm now involved in the whole research process, from producing proposals to disseminating research findings, I contribute to each aspect. This has been a gradual process: moving from data collection to analysis, then report writing and the presentation of findings, and most recently to include preparing proposals.

My degree prepared me for this position more than I realized. Only when I look back can I see that I learned the basics of carrying out a research project (from design to data collection, analysis and writing up). When I consider my role today, I see that the elements of my dissertation research project are present in all the projects I'm currently involved with.

Choosing research topics and assignment questions that will help you enter your chosen career

Even if you don't plan to go into a research post or higher degree after university, CS/ECS graduates will advise you to think hard about, say, selecting your dissertation topic area, so that you build up and can evidence the knowledge, experience and expertise you might need when it comes to looking for work. Successful graduates choose something that will give them a head start at interview, and may influence their own practice in future. The following graduate, for instance, wanted to go into teaching and to build up her knowledge of the English curriculum.

I decided to do my dissertation linked to English. I wanted to gain knowledge of new policies about teaching reading, but I focused on an aspect – shared reading – that interested me. I interviewed experienced and newly qualified teachers about how and why they used shared reading. I really got to grips with the different values and attitudes of the staff involved. I learned there was so much going on, and there are lots of approaches that have a big impact on how children learn. It gave me the chance to learn from experienced teachers: I'll certainly be including story-time for a purpose, now, because I can see how important it is. I suppose I'm much more aware of the value of reading and the importance that you have to place on it.

And here is another, who was interested in the inclusion of young children with special needs.

I knew I wanted to support childminders working with SEN children, so I did my dissertation on childminders' perceptions of quality. I compared that with OFSTED's definitions of quality. Doing this made me clearer about what makes a quality setting, so I was confident about putting forward my views about why certain practices were good and what was important to children's development when I went for my job interview.

I guess I'd already rehearsed my ideas, thought a lot about why I believed certain things, and was used to explaining the reasons for my views. They asked me about how I thought a setting should keep a child safe, and I saw it in a more complicated way than I would otherwise have done before I did my dissertation. Instead of just talking about putting child-proof locks on doors and fitting stair gates, I talked about how building effective relationships with children, where they are treated, within reason, as being able to talk about and understand what is dangerous and what keeps them safe, can have a significant impact on keeping children safe.

In both cases their dissertation choices built upon subject specific knowledge, but also allowed them to use their research to talk in considerable depth with relevant professionals, learning from their experience and gaining a genuine insight into their chosen careers. These students also used their research to reflect on and establish their own values, philosophical stance and approach to working with children. The degree allowed them the luxury of time and space to engage in such reflection before they were forced to make decisions in the challenging environment of the workplace, encumbered by professional responsibilities and obligations. Unsurprisingly, the first student went on to become, in the view of one of her PGCE tutors, 'an excellent teacher'.

Here is another example of using research to develop future professional capital. This ECS student became fascinated with issues of inclusion and entitlement with regard to young children with special educational needs during her degree. She, too, talks about using the dissertation to help her get to where she wanted to be.

I was actually amazed at how relevant my Early Childhood degree was once I started going for jobs. It turned out to be so up to date about recent approaches, which have been subject to a lot of fast-paced change, that people [in the field] were saying to me 'You're so lucky to have had the chance to spend three years studying all these things, when we have been struggling to keep abreast of it all by reading the newspapers'. So it wasn't just a case of having stuff to say and feeling confident talking about the Children Act, Every Child Matters, SureStart Children's Centres, multi-agency working, family support links with early years and so on – it was that it suddenly hit home quite how much I had to offer! That felt amazing!

When I thought about it, I'd actually written essays on all sorts of issues that have a massive impact on the world of work in early years – I'd looked at different views of quality, I'd carried out interviews with key professionals and parents, I'd visited a range of different settings – family centres, SureStart Children's Centres, nurseries, and we'd had visitors in from all of them who'd come to talk with us and share their experiences and ideas. I'd heard practitioners talk about the tensions and challenges they face in their work, how they're trying to get to grips with some of the problems man-agers face when they want to bring about change, and suddenly it drove home how relevant it all was. I mean, I know exactly how to look up infor-mation, I know the websites and that to be able to update my knowledge, for one thing. But it's more than that, really. In fact, I wish I'd been a bit more sensible and thought about this sooner, because then I'd have been more focused and made more of the opportunities on my course – made more of the essays and so on – if only I had seen the point sooner, instead of just doing assignments because I had to, just to get a mark to pass. That was, with hindsight, a bit of a waste, really – I could've made much more of it.

Building up hands-on experience

Graduates who want to work with children or take postgraduate courses will invariably find that they need to build up practical experience outside the course, as this graduate advises:

The more practical hands-on experience you get, the better, as employers will be looking for 'evidence' that you can do what you say you can do. Go beyond the course! Volunteer, babysit, work shadow, visit a range of children's serv-ices, talk to people working in the industry and attend conferences. The opportunities you take up now will shape your career.

Nowadays many full-time students need to work during their degrees, so try and make a virtue of this, as Mandy did:

During my undergraduate degree, I worked three part-time jobs as an Early Childhood Teaching Assistant, working one to one with a non-verbal 11 year old boy with autism and his family; as an Inclusion Support Worker at a school for children with autism ranging from 4 to 19 years in age; and as a Summer School Coordinator for 'gifted' 11–12 year olds.

Again, a learning log could encompass this kind of work as well as aca-demic work, outlining what skills and knowledge you have gained. Both paid work and voluntary activity can be used to build up this required prior expe-rience and, of course, this helps you to decide where you want to head, and what the requirements would be, in good time to fit it all in.

In the extract below, for instance, the advice of this graduate to students is to make sure they gain experience of working directly with children and enabling children's learning. The voluntary work also led to other opportunities, as she describes:

At a PGCE interview, obviously you need to show that you can work with and relate to children in school contexts. They want evidence of hands-on experience. That means you have to do quite a lot outside the course.

At first, I went into a school regularly, just helping out – fetching and carrying, and working with children, supporting children in their learning under the direction of the teacher. Because of my interest, the head teacher asked me to take on a specific paid role, supporting children in different classes who needed extra help with their language skills. This was a really useful experience; I saw daily school life from the inside, in lots of different classes.

It's worth remembering that you can build up valuable experience via any paid or unpaid employment you take outside your course experience as well.

The second area I used to help show my skills was my part-time job in a local supermarket. Although I originally took the job just to earn a bit of extra money, I have always been conscious that what I do there will all go towards enhancing my CV. Therefore I took on jobs such as writing the monthly newsletter for the company. I would recommend you grab any opportunities to develop your skills at work, no matter how small they may seem, as this is how you are able to sell yourself in an interview.

 key point

What jobs might I think about going into with my CS/ECS degree?

- Working with children, via careers such as teaching.
- Working for children, as in Early Years and other settings.
- Postgraduate research and other further study.
- Careers that don't involve working with children or young people. Many employers do not look for specific degree subjects, so you do need to be able to discuss your own work in relation to what they are looking for.
- Possible career areas in relation to the first two options include: education, playwork, social care, librarianship, child psychology, children's rights, SureStart, health, the voluntary sector (from large charities such as NCH or Barnardo's to smaller local organizations).

Equally, you may have discovered that you want to go into postgraduate study in the form of an MA or MSc, for instance, having become interested in specific aspects of the degree you have taken. You may also take further qualifications that will lead into specific careers, such as a PGCE, QTS or Social Work certificates, or gain an EYPS.

Your University Careers and Employment Services' website is always going to be the best place to gather information and can also offer face-to-face meetings to discuss possibilities. They will have copies of the relevant forms, a team who can field enquiries and a huge range of information about available jobs. There will also be information about funding for both part-time and full-time courses.

As mentioned above, few people arrive at university thinking about what happens after their degree. You might feel that it is too early to start thinking about careers, but previous graduates would advise you to begin immediately. Leaving it until the final year may be leaving it too late. As this graduate recalls:

> *Deciding when to start job-hunting was, perhaps surprisingly, quite a difficult decision. Going through the first two years of university it seems obvious and natural that job-hunting would begin in the third year. However, when I reached the third year I realized this may not be the best option due to the amount of work I had to do for my degree. It soon became apparent that applying for jobs would be very time consuming, and time was something that I did not really have!*
>
> *Having registered on the relevant websites, I was receiving regular emails informing me of job vacancies and many of these were the type of training schemes I was looking for. There were so many to look through I felt a bit overwhelmed and concerned about my lack of time to job hunt thoroughly. To get some advice on this I made an appointment with the careers adviser at university. I explained everything to her and she agreed that I shouldn't jeopardize my degree by spending too long applying for jobs. She suggested I pick a few key schemes that I would be really keen to get onto and apply for them. If this proved unsuccessful I could then apply to a wider range once I finished my degree. I asked whether she thought my application being for a year after I graduated rather than straight away (most have a September start) would have any effect on the success of the application and she reassured me it shouldn't make any difference. This was a great weight off my mind and I would recommend everyone visit the careers service at least once even if it is just for some reassurance that you are on the right track – job hunting seems straightforward until you set out and suddenly it gets a lot more complicated! It's good to know that there is support available and you are not on your own.*

In addition, as the graduate above suggests, using sites like http://www.prospects.ac.uk/ will help you with employment and further study. Prospects will really help you to focus on areas of interest, offering descriptions of jobs, case studies of people in those jobs and information about how to get into these areas. Sites like http://www.graduate-jobs.com/gj/index.jsp and http://targetjobs.co.uk/graduate-jobs/ will also help your search.

There are many places where jobs or graduate training schemes are advertised and sifting through them to find relevant posts can be a huge task, so start exploring now to get familiar with the field before your final year.

In addition, keep in mind that if you are intent on a specific career trajectory there will be specific sources of information. For instance, if you want to work in social care then the social care section on http://jobs.guardian.co.uk is an excellent resource. In contrast, prospective teachers should use *The Times Educational Supplement,* http://www.tes.co.uk/jobs. If you want to work for a specific local authority, their websites contain job sections. Similarly, with regard to the voluntary sector, look at the websites of specific organizations. The 'Areas of Work' section of the CWDC's site at http://www.cwdcouncil.org.uk/areas has useful information, as does Children and Young People Now, http://www.cypnow.co.uk/.

Researching an organization will help you to assess whether you want to work in it, and also help you to tailor your CV or job application. You will want to find out about the history of the organization and about how they are organized. For instance, are they local, regional or national in scope? Do they employ people from a range of professions or are they focused specifically on one area? You also need to compare them to other, similar employers regarding pay and conditions.

Even if it is early in your degree, sending off for information about jobs that you think may be part of your future can be helpful as the information pack you receive will contain not only details of the job itself but also background information on the organization and the person specification.

 to think about

If you are interested in applying for ...

MA/MSc (Master of Arts/Master of Science)

There are many reasons why you might choose to do this, from seeing further study as a route to career progression to you enjoying the challenges it offers. Talk to others to see what to expect and think through whether it would suit you.

There are specific sites which will make your search less scattershot, for instance, http://www.postgraduatestudentships.co.uk which is very thorough indeed. Also useful is http://www.jobs.ac.uk/ which has sections relating to postgraduate qualifications and funding. Alternatively, if there are specific researchers whose work interests you, find out where they are based and look at the courses offered by their institution.

The following graduate shares her reasons for her choice to return to study.

I am starting an MSc in Social Research. There are a number of reasons for this – there is little support and training for contract-researchers so any opportunity to progress and develop skills should be snapped up; I want a challenge, I want to get back to learning 'uni style', not just 'on the job' practical learning; and I want to progress up the researcher scale, so need to have a higher degree. I wouldn't personally recommend going straight from a first degree to a postgrad degree – take some time to learn through practice, suss out which postgrad course would be most beneficial to you. Oh – and ask for funding from your employer!

PGCE (Postgraduate Certificate in Education)

The PGCE is the most popular route into teaching for new graduates. Apply via the Graduate Teacher Training Registry (GTTR) at http://www.gttr.ac.uk. The initial closing date is around the 1st December although some courses may have places after this date. Applications can be made online and are processed as soon as they are received so **act early**. Primary courses fill up particularly quickly. With regard to secondary PGCE places, in order to teach in secondary schools applicants need to show a good subject knowledge related to their named subject specialism, so keep that in mind when applying.

The following account is from Carolyn, who secured a place on a PGCE. She had always known that she wanted to teach and built up a bank of knowledge to support that aim throughout her university career, particularly as she wanted to take English as her subject specialism. Here she talks about how she ensured that she took units during her course that enabled her to fulfil her aim. Her comments also emphasize the importance of thinking about the particular slant your degree has.

I always wanted to be a primary school teacher: I knew that from the begin-ning of the course. Others competing with you to get on a PGCE have sub-ject knowledge, having done a more traditional degree, like Maths or English. I felt quite daunted by that at first. So I sought advice from my Guidance Tutor, early on, and was told to broaden my knowledge base.

Then, when I was taking Childhood Studies I was very conscious that I'd need to build up a sound subject base for my teaching career. So I did what my Guidance Tutor said: I took stock of the subjects I felt good at, like English and German, and decided I had quite strong linguistic skills. So I

(Continued)

(Continued)

worked towards choosing English as my subject specialism as I went through the course, to boost that further. For example, I chose a unit on picture books and one on geography in my second year option, to give me National Curriculum subject knowledge.

SCITT (School Centred Initial Teacher Training)

SCITTS are PGCEs designed and delivered by groups of neighbouring schools and colleges. Training is more school-based as the title suggests. Application is through the GTTR or in some cases directly to the SCITT itself. Your application will not be considered if you do not show that you have some recent experience in a school or other learning setting and part of the selection process may involve being observed working with children.

Both programmes of training can lead to QTS (Qualified Teacher Status). Both the PGCE and SCITT offer similar employment prospects and, at the time of writing, have the same training bursary. For more information the Teacher Training Agency (TTA) website is a good starting point (http://www.tda.gov.uk/Recruit.aspx; Teaching Information Line 0845 6000 991).

GTP (Graduate Teacher Programme)

This is an employment-based route that was originally introduced to address the problem of filling teacher vacancies in certain subject and geographical areas. Unqualified teachers are employed by and trained in a specific school, gaining QTS this way. The scheme was introduced to attract mature entrants or those already working in a school. Entry is now open to all ages. However, the proportion of places in relation to other routes is still relatively small so applicants who have built up a wide range of experiences are preferred. For the up-to-date situation locally contact the TTA helpline (see above).

EYPS (Early Years Professional Status)

There are a number of different pathways to gain EYPS, according to your prior experience. As a graduate, individual providers will help you decide on a pathway that meets your needs, so liaise with them. A list of all training providers is available at http://www.cwdcouncil.org.uk/eyps/eyp-training-provider-details.

Alternatively, the skills that studying has given you, irrespective of subject, are going to be useful to employers, and you may want to look at going into a career which doesn't involve working with or for children or young people.

Applying for jobs and courses

CV, application forms and covering letters: the basics

It may be early in your degree, but make sure you know where your certificates, professional and other important documents are, along with any letters of support or references you have received, whether part or full time, from your school, college or employers, to ensure you can respond before application closing dates. Having this material together will help you create a CV, or fill in a form, and can act as a list of potential referees when you are writing applications.

You can apply in a number of different ways for jobs, most typically via a CV or application form. You will sometimes also need to send a covering letter. See this as a mini job application form. There is a lot of support you can tap into that will help you make the best of your knowledge and experience, as long as you have all the relevant information to hand. Your University Careers and Employment Services will be able to assist you, and tutorials are often available on creating a CV (search the relevant site using CV as a search term). In addition, you will find the CV Builder very useful at http://www.cvbuilder-advice-resources.co.uk/careersadvice/ as well as that found at http://www.prospects.ac.uk/

Most jobs will require you to fill in an application form that asks for details of your education, employment and experiences (just like a CV, but in their chosen format). Websites such as Prospects will also give helpful advice on application forms. Increasingly, application forms can be filled in online but remember how easy it is to email something that contains errors, so check the form thoroughly. Our graduates' top tip for the longer sections on the form is to complete them in a word document package first and then copy and paste them onto the actual form. Always keep a copy of the form, however it is submitted, and any research you did on the organization and job area. If you get an interview you will need to revisit all this information.

Application forms will ask for two and sometimes more references, usually from a previous employer or tutor. If your tutor would be an appropriate person, send an email explaining what you are applying for and even who you are, as they might be dealing with a large number of requests. Remember that they do not have to give a reference. If they agree, they will ask for information about the job. Send them all you can as fast as possible, including the person specification, as the time frames on references are often very short.

It might be worth bearing the following graduate's advice as you progress through your degree:

A good reference from a past lecturer is important for securing future employment. The way you present yourself and interact with others makes a statement about who you are and what you believe in, so take great care! It is the relationships and networks you forge as a student that will open doors to future employment opportunities.

CV, application forms and covering letters: issues to consider

Ensure that potential employers understand your degree   Competition in graduate employment and for further study is fierce and so CS/ECS graduates need to market their qualities carefully and explicitly. Be prepared to explain and justify your CS/ECS course on application forms and in interview when you leave university as not all employers will have a sound grasp of what these courses might actually entail. You should also highlight the particular slant of your degree, as the graduate accounts suggest. It is likely, for example, that your ECS degree will have equipped you with up-to-date knowledge of recent initiatives and approaches in the early years sector, so be sure to spell these out and highlight, say, your knowledge of the ECM agenda. Similarly, if you are a CS graduate applying for a Children's Rights Officer role, make sure you outline the ways in which you have gained knowledge and insight into children's rights policy, legislation and issues as part of your degree.

Employers may have some misperceptions of CS/ECS degrees if they are accustomed to recruiting or working with students from more vocational child-related fields. It's not uncommon for, say, head teachers, to assume that CS/ECS degrees are competency- or skills-based vocational courses. Many students actually get a first taste of these misperceptions if their course offers research observation visits to nurseries or schools. You may have found that teachers and nursery officers saw you as a student teacher on placement and so you may well be skilled already in explaining how your course differs from more 'hands-on' degrees. If not, you should think about how you will address these misconceptions when you are applying for jobs, and even when you go to visit your Careers Service.

Highlight your generic key skills   Remember that employers will see your degree in line with any other, because it represents graduate standards in key areas, such as communication, critical thinking, team-work, analysis, communication (verbal and written), project management and so on. On a CS/ECS degree the third year will typically allow you to demonstrate that you can manage your own time, make decisions, not rely exclusively upon someone else to tell you what to do, and that you know how to find out about things – in fact, all the skills and qualities of independence and decision making that employers often look for in their graduates.

The two graduates below summarize their perspectives very differently, but both emphasize the importance of these generic skills. The first says, simply:

My degree provided me with valuable experience of group work, working to deadlines, communication with people at different levels, researching, self-motivation, and presenting.

The second graduate states that:

Another worry I had was that my degree was not specific enough for the type of work I wanted. Again, I discussed this with the careers adviser and also my tutors and decided to focus all my work, especially my dissertation, on topics that related to my chosen career. The way this degree is structured allows you quite a bit of freedom to tailor it to your own needs. I was also reassured my degree would not be a problem when I started job-hunting and found that a surprising number of employers did not require specific degrees, it was more usual for them to want a 2:1 or a 2:2, or simply a 'good degree', in any subject.

You need, however, to be sure to take every opportunity to consciously develop and enhance these skills both within and outside your degree programme, as they will really count when it comes to life after university.

Degree work helped me to develop generic skills in areas such as time management, presentation skills and critical thinking. Through working with others in seminars and from practical work in schools I also developed the social skills necessary to help me find a job once I'd graduated.

During my degree I became far more confident of my ability in stressful situations (completing assignments to deadline, doing presentations with fellow undergraduates, undertaking data collection through interview for my dissertation). You'll need confidence and flexibility in work. My work involves interviewing professionals, and you definitely need to be confident in your approach, especially if you're young and female – you have to get used to patronizing tones and not let them affect you!

The person specification   The person specification can be really useful to you, as it is where the employer describes the *essential* and *desirable* criteria for the job. Every application will be assessed against these criteria and it is this process that creates the shortlist of people who will be interviewed. This is very much like writing an essay in that your tutors will have stressed that you must look at the marking criteria in order to check that you have covered all the aspects that the person marking the assignment is looking for. Present your experiences in ways that demonstrate that you meet these work-based specifications, just as you got to grips with those addressing assessed work.

This is just as important if you are applying for further training, as it is likely that the person specification will include something like, in the case of teacher training, 'direct experience of work in schools' or 'direct experience of work with children of a relevant age group'. The person specification tells you what experience you must flag up if you are to be shortlisted for courses or jobs. There is little point, then, in applying for jobs for which you do not hold the essential criteria. For some jobs there may be many people who have the essential criteria and consequently those doing the shortlisting will move to the desirable criteria as a way of sifting candidates. Make sure you also consider the desirable criteria and demonstrate your skills and your experiences in these areas too.

Person specifications will also detail the qualifications necessary for the post. These help you assess whether the jobs you are looking at match your capabilities. If the job asks for GCSE rather than degree qualifications then you might feel frustrated or bored, although it might still offer useful experience. Bear in mind, however, that you could well be seen as over-qualified. Alternatively, if you feel that you are under-qualified for the posts that you are looking at then you might have actually identified not your first post, but one that you might like to move on to, in effect mapping out your career path.

Most application forms end with a blank sheet inviting you to give further information about yourself in support of your application. You can use this in relation to the essential and desirable criteria in the person specification. Go through all of the criteria and reflect on your experiences, qualifications and the content of your course, matching what you have done against them.

You need to draw parallels between what the criteria state and what you have done. For example, one of the criteria might be 'experience of working in partnership with a variety of sectors and agencies'. You may not think that you have done this, but your university experience might well be relevant. For instance, the following shows how one graduate used her experiences at university to show how she could fulfil the criterion.

> *I understand the importance of working in partnership with a variety of different sectors and agencies. In order to do this I have made it my business to find out as much as I possibly can about the work of all the schools in the area and the various agencies that you work with such as educational psychologists, education welfare officers (EWOs), behaviour support teams, health and social services. I have carried out interviews about the challenges of partnership working with teachers and social workers and completed a special assignment on factors that make for effective partnerships in local authority settings.*

Another of the essential criteria might include, 'the ability to work well under pressure and to tight deadlines'. One graduate responded, and was successful, with the following:

Over the past three years I have successfully completed a whole range of assignments on time and to a very good standard. This has been while also holding down two part-time jobs and maintaining a long-term commitment to a local voluntary agency where I offer childcare support. This voluntary work means that I am frequently telephoned at very short notice to offer respite childcare for families in difficulty. If this happens then I have to rapidly re-schedule my other commitments in order to fulfil these responsibilities as well.

In addition, employers will often ask for skills in project management. This involves planning, monitoring and evaluating the work that you are undertaking. Your entire university career will have involved this sort of activity, including working with others in order to develop a project related to an assignment. Here is how one graduate drew on her experience in response to this criterion:

As part of my course I have frequently needed to work with others to plan out and deliver various projects. This has involved assigning tasks, setting deadlines, meeting and reviewing progress, producing the finished article whether this was a presentation or some other kind of project, receiving feedback and using this to carry out reflection and evaluation for future work.

You should always give examples of things that you have actually done to show that you meet the criteria. Responding to the criterion 'ability to establish good working relationships with all service providers' in the following way would probably not be shortlisted as the comments are too vague and woolly:

I think it is very important to develop good working relationships and I have always tried to do so. Good working relationships mean a lot to me and I like to think that I am a good colleague.

The comment offers potential employers no way of knowing whether the student has done anything that would show that they can put these desires into practice.

Similarly, a response to the criterion 'excellent interpersonal and communication skills' like the one that follows, does not offer enough information or any concrete examples:

My comunication skills are great! Everybody says so! Im a good talker and an even better listener.

There is no reference to any kinds of communication other than speaking and listening. The ability to communicate in writing, by email, in reports, and so on is similarly important. In addition, the response does not demonstrate the ability to use different sorts of registers – ways of addressing an audience – for different circumstances. The approach above is far too informal for a letter of application.

Finally, the basic spelling mistakes and typos in the above responses might suggest to a potential employer that there is a big gap between this person's perception of themselves and their actual ability when it comes to interpersonal and communication skills.

The job specification   The job specification lists a series of duties and responsibilities associated with the post. The specification below is a typical example, and the following discussion focuses on how you might go about applying for this post, and how your degree might be used to provide evidence that you are the person for the job.

Again, when you see one of these documents it is important to consider the criteria in relation to the knowledge, skills and values that you have gained at university. If you were to apply for this post, you would need to go through each of the units or modules you have covered on your course and list the relevant knowledge you have gained.

 case study

A typical job specification

Community Engagement Worker: SureStart Children's Centre £19,770–22,971

- The post requires energy and enthusiasm to enable families of under 4s to access better childcare, health care and education.
- To work with parents, carers and community representatives to enable the identification of local needs and to develop services that respond to those needs.
- To devise strategies and approaches to ensure the involvement of hard to reach families and children in the catchment area.

Duties and responsibilities

- To work to the SureStart Children's Centre ethos to implement a community engagement strategy, which ensures the process of ongoing community participation in the region.

- To ensure the involvement of hard to reach families in the SureStart Children's Centre catchment area.
- To liaise with families, other key workers and relevant organizations.
- To help develop support groups and family support networks.
- To monitor achievement against the SureStart Children's Centre targets and outcomes.
- To provide broad-based advice and guidance to families of under 4s.
- To link local, regional and national initiatives in a strategic way.
- To research, develop and prepare funding applications.
- To produce reports as required under the terms and conditions of the programme.
- To support and assist in the development of childcare facilities and services.
- Work as part of a SureStart Children's Centre integrated team.
- Any other duties as may be required by the Programme Manager.

Knowledge   You could, for instance, think about what you know about the organization, asking yourself whether you know what a SureStart Children's Centre is, how it evolved and how it is funded. There is also the wider, political context. Ask yourself what you know about the development of childcare, the legislation involved and the various issues related to looking for good quality childcare. What have you learnt about the way in which government policy has responded to the childcare challenge, and how has it been linked to other agendas, such as regeneration and anti-poverty? What knowledge have you gained about the challenges inherent in this agenda: lack of time, resources, issues around access and so on?

Other relevant knowledge will be about children and families. Ask yourself what you know about development needs and the different perspectives about children's needs. Consider how you have begun to explore and analyse the various perspectives of professionals, parents and children themselves, as that will help you to tune in to different stakeholders' perceptions of what is in the best interests of children. What debates have you been introduced to in relation to families with particular difficulties or access issues or special educational needs?

In addition, there are aspects of how you gained this knowledge about SureStart that might be useful to think through when applying for this job. For instance, a key question is *how* do you know what you know? Has it been through talking and listening to key stakeholders, through reading and research, through observation, or any other methods?

There are also issues about professional practice here. For instance, what has your course taught you about the challenges and tensions embedded in multi-disciplinary working? What has it taught you about different professional perspectives and the challenges of enabling people to work outside of their particular professional boxes? What have you learnt about professional cultures and the power of different professions and the role of professions and professionals within society? Have you been exposed to different environments where professionals work and has this helped you to gain an understanding of different cultures and contexts?

Finally, you could think through which assignments you have done that have helped you to unpack these issues and whether your course has introduced you to ethical issues related to collecting information and presenting it in different formats.

Skills The next stage is to consider what relevant skills you have. For instance, your degree will have honed your ability to consider different perspectives on issues and attitudes. Here you can draw on assignments where you did well or where you tackled a relevant topic area for this particular post. This could include assignments where you interviewed someone with a responsibility for children's care or education, such as professionals working in the community.

Collating and organizing information gathered either from books, journals or from talking to relevant individuals and producing essays and reports as a result will have given you skills in both writing and researching. These skills can also be used to gather information that can help you prepare funding applications. Even if you have never prepared one of these before you have learnt how to use the Web, how to sort out authoritative sources from those that cannot be trusted and how to carry out investigations to narrow down fields of enquiry to a really focused end.

You may also have had to produce a draft or a proposal for your dissertation, if you had to do one. In doing so you will have convinced your tutors that you had a good understanding of the scope of the project and of the resources needed. This is very like a research bid. Further, this can be seen to demonstrate time management and project management skills. These will also have been demonstrated through your completion of other assignments where you planned and managed your own learning.

Finally, you will have developed your collaborative skills, for example by undertaking group presentations or negotiating access to settings or individuals.

Values and beliefs Any employer will look at an application form hoping to find some assurance that you have values and beliefs which mean you will fit into their team.

In relation to this, your course will have given you opportunities to examine your beliefs about children and children's needs, making you very self-aware. In addition, you will have learnt to argue your case and present your reasons for your beliefs or actions clearly.

You will also be able to recognize the way in which people's attitudes are related to their professional training, personal experiences, upbringing and culture. Alongside this will be an awareness of the need to be non-judgmental and tolerant of other people's opinions.

Further, you will have had to address issues around equality of opportunity and children's rights and those who are often seen as under-represented such as people with special educational needs or from minority ethnic groups.

In responding to the job description, then, you will need to show that you have an awareness of the challenges inherent in representing a range of different views and ideas.

 **key point**

Knowledge: stress the fact that you are up to date with recent and relevant information around legislation, child development, topical issues, social care, education issues and children's rights.

Skills: stress the fact you have learnt to research, study, analyse, problem solve, communicate, organize, discuss, prioritize, listen and debate.

Values and beliefs: stress the fact that you are flexible, child centred, open and tolerant, and have an awareness of different opinions and a commitment to equal opportunities.

Interviews and presentations: the basics

Getting to interview means that you have shown the staff doing the short-listing that you can fulfil the criteria on the job specification and the person specification, at least enough for them to want to meet you face to face. If you have been shortlisted you will receive a letter giving you the time and date of your interview along with a map, details of how to get to the venue and a contact number for you to confirm you are going to attend (it will make a good impression to do so).

You now need to think about how you are going to perform well. To begin with, reread the copy of the application form that you made, to remind yourself of what you said. Gather together all the material you can about the organization – something that will be fairly easy, as you will have done some research already. You will also find that leaflets like 'Preparing for Interviews', available from the careers service, give checklists that will help you with both preparation and the etiquette of interviews, for instance remembering to thank interviewers for their time and what to wear (as first impressions do count).

A key tip from our graduates is about making sure that you know exactly where the interview is to take place. If at all possible do a dry run so that you know the public transport routes, or, if you are going by car, where you can park and whether you will need appropriate change for a machine. You should be at the venue at least 15 minutes before you are actually due to give yourself time to settle. One graduate also suggests having the phone numbers for the potential employer given to you on the interview letter programmed into your mobile, so that if you find you are unavoidably going to be late you can call and explain what is happening.

Most interviews will consist of a series of questions that will be delivered by each member of the interview panel, usually in turn. There should be the same initial questions to each candidate. While you are answering these questions it is quite common for the interviewers to be scribbling comments. This can be off-putting, but is necessary to enable them to judge who is the best candidate. Concentrate solely on what you want to say.

Candidates will often be asked to prepare a short presentation to deliver before interview. If this is the case, the letter offering you an interview will give you a title which you are to present upon. You will also be told how long the presentation is to last and whether there is any technology available that you can use. If PowerPoint or overhead projectors (OHPs) are available then you will need to decide if you *want* to use them (as the other candidates may), and be confident that you know *how* to use them.

Your presentation should be rehearsed both in front of a mirror and to an audience. This will allow you to practise giving appropriate eye contact and hopefully help you get over any fears you may have. As this graduate suggests, however, your experience of giving presentations will prove useful:

Presentation skills in particular helped me to get my job, as it involves training groups of people and holding full-day inductions – no matter how much I hated doing presentations in first year it has certainly paid off!

key point

Some of the basic requirements of a presentation are that you should:

- Keep to time. If for any reason you do run out of time, take a breath, summarize in a sentence and finish. Do not substantially over-run or under-run.

- Ensure all of your slides or overheads are clearly visible and contain only the essential information.
- Have notes that you are comfortable with handling (small cards tied together work well).
- Make sure you look at your audience, smile and pace yourself so that your words are not garbled.
- Position yourself so that you are not blocking anybody's view of the slides (if you decide to use them) and ensure that you do not have your back to any member of the audience.

Remember that everybody is nervous in interviews so the panel will expect some hesitation and nervousness and try to put you at ease.

Interviews and presentations: issues to consider

Why you?   Usually, interviews will include a variation on the theme of 'why do think we should give you this job?' Even if this question is not asked directly it is really important to have rehearsed in your own mind why you should be appointed to the post, by thinking through what skills and knowledge you can bring to it.

In relation to both application forms and interviews graduates will return time and again to the *issues* that their course made them engage with and how this was a key element of their success in demonstrating that they were the best candidate.

When I went for my interview I had lots to say. They asked me, for instance, to tell them about an episode in which I had taught a child in school, and how I approached that. They wanted to know what I knew about how children learn, how I would structure activities, how I would respond to them, and help them progress. As well as having direct experience from what I'd done in my own time, I had also thought about these things as part of my course. For example, if I'd have read Granpa *to children without having done the 'Picturebooks and Developing Readers' option unit, I would have just gone through it, reading it as just a story to read at storytime, and that would be it. Now, having looked at how it works, and what kinds of things it's doing, I can see how there are lots of interesting things I can do with it.*

That happened as well, when the head teacher on the interview panel asked me to talk about how I'd work with parents. I could talk about a Parents into Schools initiative I'd seen when I was working in school, but I realized I actually knew a lot too, from Perspectives on Parenting, about not being judgmental and making people feel 'bad' parents. So I talked about making them feel welcome in school, and helping them to understand what is being covered in school, and generally working in partnership together. I could easily talk about these things, as they were issues we covered on the course.

Interviews are a kind of performance and the graduate above, with her genuine passion and knowledge of issues, engaged the interviewers and gave herself a good chance of getting the post. You also need to come across as an enthusiastic, committed and positive potential member of staff.

Make sure you tell employers about both your course-related and generic skills
The skills you develop on your CS/ECS course may be specifically related to certain types of future employment. For example, this graduate, who secured a job as an advocate for young people, drew upon the children's rights element of her course to highlight her suitability for the post. She also drew upon what she called the 'people skills' she developed as part of her course, such as working with others, developing the confidence to express her views and persuade other people, and presentation skills (which can also be marketed as generic skills). She saw this as a matter of trying to understand and respect other people's perspectives, values and attitudes. This now underpins the way she carries out her work and informs how she approaches and deals with young people. In other words, she had learnt to articulate and explain the value of her particular CS course, and the importance of the values, attitudes and approaches that were fostered within it.

I have gained a great deal from the course that is relevant for working with any kind of person. I find myself thinking about the ways in which we work with people, and questioning presumptions made about their lives. Rather than making decisions on their behalf, I am keen to give the participants the lead in making choices about their futures through feedback and discussion groups, as well as simply providing an environment in which they feel able to express their views.

You can also highlight your child-centred values, as this graduate, a teacher, does:

Above all, though, CS helped me to understand why children may behave or react in the ways that they do, and I know I treat them with respect as individuals.

Or as this graduate, a PGCE student, does:

I think I'll be a better teacher having done Childhood Studies because I understand children as people, and see the whole child. I think I'm more likely to make an effort to listen and take children seriously, although I know there'll be pressures that will mean that's quite difficult to achieve. But at least forewarned is forearmed. I feel I've got a broader picture about the education system and children's roles within it to hang onto, especially when I'm starting out.

Reflecting on your course and relating it to the relevant sector   Make sure you take stock of the relevance of the subjects you are studying and think positive for both application forms and interviews! Again, a learning log might be useful.

I felt quite daunted going for my PGCE interview, because I don't have a normal subject degree. But when I thought about it, I realized that I'd got other skills and knowledge to offer. I had a lot of knowledge about children and how they learn. I knew more than anyone else going for interview about child development, for example. I know an awful lot about how and when children generally learn to achieve things, so I think that'll help me be realistic in my expectations of children, and I talked about how that would help me in a teacher's role.

I'd also done a lot of units that were directly relevant to teaching, and gave me a broader view of education and school. Schooling in Childhood gave me a broad overview of the National Curriculum, special needs, the history of how schools came to be as they are, how they are run, school governors, about OFSTED, Children's Services, general policy and practice overview – all sorts of useful things like that. I found having that broad overview was important at the interview, knowing about the issues.

We also did a unit on children's learning on Childhood Studies. I learned about different teaching approaches, and learning styles. I looked particularly at assessment, which is a massive issue in schools now. I became interested in children's self-evaluation skills, and consulting with children is very much being promoted now. For my coursework activities, which built up to that assignment, I interviewed a teacher about the ways she uses annotated work in English, Maths and Science. It was all about giving the child a voice, and to help them think about their learning. That gave me ideas for strategies I might use when I become a teacher, and I learned that children can make decisions, if they're asked. Before I wouldn't have thought like that. I'd have thought teachers should do that for them. So I guess the course just made me think, be a bit more open to trying out ideas for getting children involved in learning, which is a big issue nowadays: how to involve children.

Questions from you   At the end of the interview you will be asked if you have any questions for the panel. It is always good to have one or two to hand, but you will need to think about the impression that the questions you choose to ask give of you. Ask a question that enhances something that you have been told already shows your willingness to develop and grow into the job. A good question, for example, could be, *'are there opportunities for further development and a chance to take on new initiatives?'*, or alternatively, *'could you give me some idea of the kind of induction that you would be offering for the post to the successful candidate?'*

If you genuinely do not have a question then say so, but word it carefully. Something like *'everybody's been so helpful today that all my questions have been answered'* suggests that you have valued and appreciated the information that you have been given, while a simple *'no'* actually sounds rather too blunt, even if it is true.

Alternative selection processes for graduate schemes

Some of our graduates apply for jobs where the selection process involves much more than interview and presentation. It's worth finding out about these in advance from the Careers Service. Only apply if you feel confident of handling both the job and selection procedure. If you're fazed by the selection procedures you possibly wouldn't enjoy the job. One graduate described her experience of an alternative selection process as follows:

For the first stage I went down to London for a residential. After an interview I had to take part in a group exercise. I think this lasted about 40 minutes and involved six of us reading a scenario and then working through it. We were each given a different role to play and had to act out a meeting in which we were deciding how to prioritize various issues that needed to be looked at within a fictional working situation. We each had our own issue to put forward and of course all of us were trying to get ours to be the top priority.

It was quite an intense and tiring day but I actually enjoyed much of it. It might sound daft saying try and enjoy the experience but at the end of the day you are either going to get it or you're not and it's not the end of the world if you don't. Being worried and nervous will not help and in fact will probably lessen your chances of being successful as I found out in the final stage.

Having been successful in the interview and group exercise, I was invited to attend a 24-hour assessment at a Conference Centre. This was testing how well you would cope in the role of a manager. We were each given a desk with a laptop and printer and all the activities were sent via email to the laptop. These included writing reports and attending meetings. The reports were testing how well you could assimilate a lot of information received during a short space of time and in a variety of forms, for example one exercise included a graph showing the predicted costs of building work, the requirements of those who would be using the building, budgets, predicted user numbers, etc. It was then my job to put all this information together into a proposal about what should be done, what the cost would be, and whether or not it could be done within the budget provided.

With only 40 minutes to get through all the information and complete the report I found this extremely difficult. There were also three meetings to attend: one with a colleague, one with a group of colleagues and a representative from another organization, and one with a medical consultant. As with the report, a great deal of information was emailed prior to attending each meeting and this needed to be read, understood and the main points pulled out to be used in the meetings. I found my nerves got the better of me and I panicked due to the vast amount of information I was expected to take in. If I was to go back and do this assessment again I would put in a lot more time preparing for it. I thought I couldn't really prepare as I did not know what to expect; however, speaking to other candidates who had attended other assessments with different organizations I discovered it was quite a common structure. Knowing this, I think I could have made better use of the careers service who do offer help in preparing for this kind of assessment centre.

Making the most of feedback

If everything has gone well then you get the best feedback of all – hearing that you have got the job. However, given the competitive nature of the job market, it may be that you miss out. If that is the case, you can ask for feedback on your performance. Almost any organization will be happy to give you feedback and you need to take it in the spirit in which it is intended, namely that it should be seen as a way of helping you to do better next time.

Seek feedback on what went well as well as on how you could improve. Your letter of application was strong and that will be why you were interviewed, but it may be that you needed more experience or that some of your answers indicated that you needed more knowledge about some aspects of the role.

Write down the feedback that you get and think about it seriously. Plan two or three things that you can do and give yourself a time frame as to when you are going to do them. Share the feedback with people that you trust who are in a position to help you.

The feedback may suggest that you had appropriate knowledge and skills but that your values or attitudes differed from those of the organization concerned. Just because you did not fit this time does not mean that you will not fit in with another organization, so persist. The interview process allows those interviewing to gauge whether they think somebody would fit into the culture of an organization and be happy in it, not just whether someone can do the job.

Where are they now?

Following graduation CS/ECS students go into a diverse range of roles, and not all of them will work with, or even for, children or young people. However, a good number do go on to teach in primary schools, or to manage or co-ordinate services or projects for children or adolescents, or to work with parents and families, or are employed in Children's Services, and a few go on to do childhood-related research. Find out what sort of jobs people from your course have gone into, as it may prompt you to think about new possibilities.

Examples of the varied future career paths our own graduates have taken include:

- Area Development Officer for Children's Services
- Children's Rights Officer
- Parent and Toddler Group Support Worker
- Extended Services through Schools Officer
- Family support worker
- Primary teacher
- Parent Participation worker employed by voluntary sector providers
- Children's Centre childcare manager
- Speech and language therapy support worker
- FE lecturer
- Asylum seekers/homeless families officer
- Education Liaison Officer working at the interface between schools/colleges and universities
- Nursery Manager
- Learning Mentor (special needs)
- Play co-ordinator
- Connexions Personal Adviser
- Manager of children's respite services
- Postgraduate Certificate in Education (PGCE)
- Diploma in Social Work
- Children's publishing
- Family Learning Co-ordinator within Children's Services
- OFSTED Registered Inspector
- Children's Trust Co-ordinator
- Training and Development officer: Housing
- Senior Research Assistant working in a university research unit
- MA/MSc degrees in Social Research, Social Policy, Social Work, Childhood Studies, Psychology
- Human Resource Management.

CS/ECS students' first destinations following their degree

You can read about some of the opportunities taken up by CS/ECS students immediately after they finished their courses below (these complement the ones you can find above). Each gives you a feel for the work, an idea of what it entails, and their views on why and how they chose to follow that particular route.

Education Liaison Officer   On leaving university Heather went to work for another university's student recruitment office. Her job mainly involved delivering talks to Year 12 students in local colleges and schools and was targeted at young people whose socio-economic backgrounds meant that they were unlikely to think about attending university. Heather's job was to:

- raise awareness about the benefits of higher education
- help youngsters see what student life was really like
- generally raise the aspirations and confidence of young people in the region
- encourage them to consider applying to university.

The initiative that funded her post also put together a range of activity days and residential visits designed to offer a taste of student life. These included:

- running subject taster sessions
- study skills activities
- facilitating the shadowing of current university students
- allowing young people the chance to participate in summer schools that enabled them to demonstrate their potential to be successful university students.

Although Heather initially started her CS course thinking that she would like to work with younger children, during the degree she found she actually enjoyed working with older children and young adults, although this was something she hadn't considered at all before coming to university. In her comments about this job she places a lot of emphasis on reflecting on people's values, children's voices and the critical thinking skills she has developed as part of her degree, which she now draws upon in her professional role:

I am working with schools and colleges from areas with high levels of need, who by their nature do not have the special advantages that many people take for granted. Childhood Studies did open my eyes to the diversity of children's experiences and educational circumstances and made me think about my reaction towards them. Working with children as research participants during the Childhood Studies degree made me think critically about how the project's aims could be achieved. I helped to develop feedback from the youngsters taking part in the project, and especially built on the research methods we'd explored that try to overcome the power imbalance in the adult–child relationship, so young people could have a say.

Research Assistant   Sarah wasn't entirely sure what she wanted to do when she left university although she had always enjoyed and been good at academic study. She considered going into postgraduate study, but at this stage, funding a higher degree proved to be quite a challenge.

I left uni with very little idea of where I wanted to be; I really wanted to go on to further studies but couldn't afford it and, looking back, I'm glad I didn't go straight into a higher degree as I have come to appreciate how much I am able to learn in employment. I was very lucky getting my first job in research; my dissertation supervisor at uni contacted me, asking if I was interested in doing some research for a Midlands university (I had no prior paid research experience), evaluating a preschool programme for literacy. My dissertation had focused on a similar subject, looking at a preschool initiative encouraging parents to share books with babies – this is why my dissertation supervisor thought I might be interested. I'm very, very grateful to her for suggesting I apply for this research position – this post confirmed for me research was a career I would like to pursue.

After this short-term research position, I became a Research Assistant at the Sustainable Cities Research Institute. I was initially employed to evaluate two SureStart programmes. My employer was keen for me to develop my understanding across various disciplines within Sustainable Cities, assigning me to a variety of projects, including: a credit union feasibility study, a handyperson scheme feasibility study, a local authority health theme evaluation, a local inquiry into citizen participation, an evaluation of a crèche training course, and an Identification, Referral and Tracking (IRT) pilot evaluation. As well as gaining an understanding of a range of subject areas, this has enabled me to work alongside a number of researchers of different levels, each with a particular style and range of skills, which has been of great benefit to me.

My day-to-day activities are varied – it depends which project I'm working on at the time and the stage I am at with it. I can be working on three different projects so could be involved in the proposal stage, project design, literature search and review, data collection, progress reports/feedback meetings, analysis, report writing, presentations.

With this work, although the project may have a team of researchers, essentially you're on your own. Out and about a lot, doing interviews all over

– so, get used to public transport; as a researcher, you're on it a lot! Also, brush up on your map-reading skills – interviews generally take place at participants' workplaces, which could be anywhere!

You can feel isolated as a researcher – you need to be able to motivate yourself, even when working on a project which can be very boring! Also, you need to be aware of your limits and ask for help and support if you need it.

Inclusion Worker   When Sue left university she wanted to work to support families with young children with special needs. When she successfully applied for the post of Inclusion Worker, her work placed her in a team of officers who worked closely with the voluntary sector.

Her day-to-day job involved working with and in playgroups where there were young children who needed one-to-one support in order to access the activities alongside other children. She also worked with other professionals, such as speech therapists, physiotherapists and educational psychologists to assess children's needs, thus ensuring that their move to nursery or school was successful.

I was always very committed to inclusive practice for children with special educational needs. Playgroups are the first place that a parent with a child with SEN leaves that child in the care of 'stranger', and that's a big step for everyone in the family to take. So my role involves me getting to know the child and building up the confidence of the parents, so that they feel reassured that their child will be safe in the new setting.

A final word

We very much hope that you find our book useful and that you enjoy your course to the full.

to think about

We'd like to finish by handing over to one of our most successful students, who looks back over her experience in order to offer what seems extremely important advice:

(Continued)

(Continued)

The main thing I have learnt through all these experiences is to keep a record of everything you do and look upon everything as experience and improving your employability. Some things may seem irrelevant or not important, but you never know when an opportunity may arise that will require you to draw on what you have already done and put those skills into practice. Above all, use the support available – careers service, tutors, websites, and friends. They may have been through similar experiences and can offer advice, or you may ask them to proof-read an application form, or maybe they are just a shoulder to cry on or someone to celebrate with!

Good luck – we wish you every success!

Further Reading and Resources

The following are useful general texts on the subject of childhood or early childhood, although this list is by no means exhaustive. Nearly all of these authors have written other books which you might also find useful, but many more obviously exist. You'll need, of course, to follow up more specialized reading lists on your own course.

Abbott, L. and Langston, A. (2004) *Birth to Three Matters: Supporting the Framework of Effective Practice*. Maidenhead: Open University Press.

Abbott, L. and Langston, A. (eds) (2006) *Parents Matter: Supporting the Birth to Three Matters Framework*. Maidenhead: Open University Press.

Anning, A., Cottrell, D., Frost, N. and Robinson, M. (2006) *Developing Multiprofessional Teamwork for Integrated Children's Services: Research, Policy and Practice*. Maidenhead: OUP.

Anning, A., Cullen, J. and Fleer, M. (eds) (2008) *Early Childhood Education: Society and Culture* (2nd edition). London: Sage.

Baldock, P., Fitzgerald, D. and Kay, J. (2009) *Understanding Early Years Policy* (2nd edition). London: Sage.

Barker, R. (ed.) (2008) *Making Sense of Every Child Matters: Multi-professional Practice Guidance*. London: Policy Press.

Bell, J. (2005) *Doing Your Research Project: A Guide for First-time Researchers in Education, Health and Social Science* (4th edition). Maidenhead: OUP.

Bruce, T. (2005) *Early Childhood Education* (3rd edition). London: Hodder Arnold.

Buckingham, D. (2000) *After the Death of Childhood: Growing Up in the Age of Electronic Media*. Cambridge: Polity.

Christensen, P. and James, A. (2007) *Research with Children: Perspectives and Practices*. London: Routledge.

Corsaro, W. (2005) *The Sociology of Childhood* (2nd edition). London: Sage.

Fitzgerald, D. and Kay, J. (2007) *Working Together in Children's Services*. London: David Fulton.

Foley, P. and Rixon, A. (eds) (2008) *Changing Children's Services: Working and Learning Together*. London: Policy Press.

Greene, S. and Hogan, D. (eds) (2005) *Researching Children's Experience: Approaches and Methods*. London: Sage.

Hallett, C. and Prout, A. (2003) *Hearing the Voices of Children: Social Policy for a New Century*. London: RoutledgeFalmer.

Holt, J. (1975) *Escape from Childhood: The Needs and Rights of Children*. Harmondsworth: Penguin.

Hutchby, I. and Moran- Ellis, J. (2001) *Children, Technology and Culture: The Impacts of Technologies in Children's Everyday Lives.* London: RoutledgeFalmer.

James, A. and James, A. (2008) *Key Concepts in Childhood Studies.* London: Sage.

James, A. and Prout, A. (eds) (1997) *Constructing and Reconstructing Childhood: Contemporary Issues in the Sociological Study of Childhood* (2nd edition). London: Falmer.

James, A., Jenks, C. and Prout, A. (1998) *Theorizing Childhood.* Cambridge: Polity Press.

Jenks, C. (1996) *Childhood.* London: Routledge.

Jones, P. (2009) *Rethinking Childhood: Attitudes in Contemporary Society.* London: Continuum.

Kehily, M. J. (ed.) (2008) *An Introduction to Childhood Studies* (2nd edition). Maidenhead: Open University Press.

Lee, N. (2001) *Childhood and Society: Growing Up in an Age of Uncertainty.* Buckingham: Open University Press.

Levin, P. (2005) *Excellent Dissertations!* Maidenhead: OUP.

Lindon, J. (2005) *Understanding Child Development: Linking Theory and Practice.* London: Hodder Arnold.

Mayall, B. (ed.) (1994) *Children's Childhoods: Observed and Experienced.* London: Falmer Press.

Mayall, B. (2002) *Towards a Sociology for Childhood: Thinking from Children's Lives.* Buckingham: Open University Press.

Maynard, T. and Thomas, N. (2004) *An Introduction to Early Childhood Studies.* London: Sage.

Mills, J. and Mills, R. (eds) (2000) *Childhood Studies: A Reader in Perspectives of Childhood.* London: Routledge.

Mitchell, H., Wild, M. and Swarbrick, N. (2007) *Early Childhood Studies Reflective Reader.* Exeter: Learning Matters.

Moon, J. (2009) *Making Groups Work: Improving Group Work through the Principles of Academic Assertiveness in Higher Education and Professional Development.* Bristol. HEA ESCalate.

Moyles, J. (2006) *Just Playing. The Role and Status of Play in Early Childhood Education.* Buckingham: Open University Press.

Nutbrown, C. (2005) *Key Concepts in Early Childhood Education and Care.* London: Sage.

Penn, H. (2008) *Understanding Early Childhood: Issues and Controversies* (2nd edition). Maidenhead: OUP.

Postman, N. (1983) *The Disappearance of Childhood: How TV is Changing Children's Lives.* London: W. H. Allen.

Pugh, G. and Duffy, B. (eds) (2006) *Contemporary Issues in the Early Years: Working Collaboratively for Children* (4th edition). London: Sage.

Roberts, R. (2002) *Self-Esteem and Early Learning* (2nd edition). London: Paul Chapman.

Roberts-Holmes, G. (2005) *Doing Your Early Years Research Project: A Step by Step Guide.* London: Sage.

Saraj- Blatchford, M., Clarke, K. and Needham, M. (eds) (2007) *The Team Around the Child: Multi-agency Working in the Early Years.* Stoke-on-Trent: Trentham Books.

Scraton, P. (ed.) (1997) *Childhood In Crisis.* London: UCL Press.

Stainton Rogers, R. and Stainton Rogers, W. (1992) *Stories of Childhood: Shifting Agendas of Child Concern.* Hemel Hempstead: Harvester Wheatsheaf.

Taylor, J. and Woods, M. (1998) *Early Childhood Studies: An Holistic Introduction.* London: Arnold.

Waller, T. (ed.) (2005) *An Introduction to Early Childhood: A Multi-disciplinary Approach.* London: Paul Chapman Press.

Willan, J., Parker-Rees, R. and Savage, J. (eds) (2007) *Early Childhood Studies* (2nd edition). Exeter: Learning Matters.

Wyness, M. (2006) *Childhood and Society: An Introduction to the Sociology of Childhood.* London: Palgrave MacMillan.

Wyse, D. (2003) *Childhood Studies: An Introduction.* London: Blackwell.

Zwozdiak-Myers, P. (2007) *Childhood and Youth Studies* (2nd edition). Exeter: Learning Matters.

Further indicative online resources

Again, the following websites are designed purely to give you a start, and we have grouped them under common themes. They are by no means exhaustive and you should follow up specific specialist sites suggested by your own tutors.

Education/schools

Advisory Centre for Education (ACE) www.ace-ed.org.uk/

Booktrust http://www.booktrust.org.uk/Home

Department for Children, Schools and Families http://www.dcsf.gov.uk/

Department for Children, Schools and Families. Standards Site http://www.standards.dcsf.gov.uk/

The General Teaching Council for Northern Ireland http://www.gtcni.org.uk/

Learning and Teaching Scotland http://www.ltscotland.org.uk/

National Curriculum www.nc.uk.net/home.html

The National Grid for Learning Cymru (NGfL Cymru) http://www.ngfl-cymru.org.uk/index-new.htm

The National Institute of Adult Continuing Education (NIACE) http://www.niace.org.uk/ (taking over the work of Basic Skills Agency along with Tribal, see below).

National Literacy Trust www.literacytrust.org.uk/

The National Strategies on the web http://nationalstrategies.standards.dcsf.gov.uk/

Office for Standards in Education (OFSTED) www.ofsted.gov.uk/

Qualifications and Curriculum Authority (QCA) www.qca.org.uk/

Teachernet http://www.teachernet.gov.uk/

Tribal http://www.tribalgroup.co.uk/servicesandsectors/Pages/education.aspx

Research

Assessment Reform Group (ARG) http://www.assessment-reform-group.org/

Centre for Studies on Inclusive Education http://www.csie.org.uk/

Effective Provision of Preschool Education Project (EPPE) http://eppe.ioe.ac.uk/

Joseph Rowntree Foundation Research http://www.jrf.org.uk/

National Foundation for Educational Research (NFER) http://www.nfer.ac.uk/index.cfm

Online journal searching services, e.g. http://www.intute.ac.uk/socialsciences/socialwelfare/

Voluntary agencies

These vary, some being large charity organizations, including:

Action for Children http://www.actionforchildren.org.uk/
Barnardos www.barnardos.org.uk/
Child Poverty Action Group www.cpag.org.uk
Childline www.childline.org.uk/
The Children's Society http://www.childrenssociety.org.uk/
Contact a Family www.cafamily.org.uk
Coram www.coram.org.uk/
Daycare Trust www.daycaretrust.org.uk/
Homestart http://www.home-start.org.uk/
Joseph Rowntree Foundation www.jrf.org.uk
National Children's Bureau www.childpolicy.org.uk
National Children's Bureau Child Bereavement Network (CBN) www.ncb.org.uk/cbn/
National Society for the Prevention of Cruelty to Children (NSPCC) www.nspcc.org.uk
Save the Children www.savethechildren.org/

And more specialized charities, such as:

MENCAP http://www.mencap.org.uk/landing.asp?id=8
Parents for the Early intervention of Autism (PEACH) www.peach.org.uk/Home/
SCOPE http://www.scope.org.uk/index.shtml

There are, though, many smaller local voluntary agencies, too numerous to list.

Family support

Centre for Fun and Families http://www.funandfamilies.co.uk/index.html
Children's National Service Framework http://www.dh.gov.uk/en/Healthcare/Children/
   NationalServiceFrameworkdocuments/index.htm
Families need Fathers www.fnf.org.uk/
Gingerbread www.gingerbread.org.uk/
National Academy for Parenting Practitioners www.parentingacademy.org/
Parenting UK http://www.parentinguk.org/
Parentline Plus http://www.parentlineplus.org.uk/
Parents Centre http://www.parentscentre.gov.uk/

Young people

Aiming High for Young People http://www.dcsf.gov.uk/everychildmatters/Youth/
   aiminghigh/aiminghigh/
British Youth Council www.byc.org.uk/
Connexions Direct http://www.connexions-direct.com/index.cfm
A National Voice (for young care leavers) www.anationalvoice.org/
School COUNCILS UK http://www.schoolcouncils.org/

Teenage Pregnancy Strategy (DCSF) http://www.dcsf.gov.uk/everychildmatters/
healthandwellbeing/teenagepregnancy/teenagepregnancy/
Youth Matters http://www.dcsf.gov.uk/everychildmatters/Youth/youthmatters/
youthmatters/

Early Years

Bookstart www.bookstart.co.uk/
British Association for Early Education www.early-education.org.uk/
ChildcareLink www.childcarelink.gov.uk
The Children's Workforce Development Council (CWDC) http://www.cwdcouncil.org.uk/
Department for Children, Schools and Families http://www.dcsf.gov.uk/index.htm
Early Years and Childcare http://www.dcsf.gov.uk/everychildmatters/earlyyears/
The Early Years Foundation Stage http://www.standards.dfes.gov.uk/eyfs/
Every Child Matters http://www.dcsf.gov.uk/everychildmatters/
High Scope www.high-scope.org.uk
National Childminding Association http://www.ncma.org.uk/MainWebSite/Homepageb51465f4.
aspx?Map=163EB4336F1F8E141AF4FDF3DCD0FDA9
National Day Nursery Association www.ndna.org.uk
Preschool Learning Alliance (playgroups) www.pre-school.org.uk
SureStart Children's Centres http://www.dcsf.gov.uk/everychildmatters/earlyyears/surestart/
whatsurestartdoes/
Surestart (archived site) www.surestart.gov.uk/

Children's rights

Centre for Europe's Children http://www.cridoc.net/centre_for_europes_children.php
Child's Rights Information Network www.crin.org/
Childwatch www.childwatch.uio.no/
Commission for Equality and Human Rights http://www.equalityhumanrights.com/
Education Otherwise www.education-otherwise.org/
National Children's Bureau http://www.ncb.org.uk/about_us.aspx
UK Youth Parliament www.ukyouthparliament.org.uk/
UN Convention on the Rights of the Child www.ohchr.org/english or www.unhchr.
ch/html/menu2/6/crc/treaties/crc.htm
UNICEF www.unicef.org

Libraries and information services

Connexions Direct http://www.connexions-direct.com/index.cfm
Early Years Library Network http://www.cilip.org.uk/specialinterestgroups/bysubject/
youth
Museums, Libraries and Archives Council http://www.mla.gov.uk/
School Libraries Group http://www.cilip.org.uk/specialinterestgroups/bysubject/school
School Libraries Association http://www.sla.org.uk/

Seven Stories: The Centre for Children's Books http://www.sevenstories.org.uk/home/
  index.php
Youth Libraries Group (YLG) http://www.cilip.org.uk/specialinterestgroups/bysubject/
  youth

Policies and legislation

2020 Children and Young People's Workforce Strategy http://www.dcsf.gov.uk/
  everychildmatters/strategy/childrenandyoungpeoplesworkforce/workforcestrategy/
Bills Before Parliament (search the site using Child or Children as search terms) http://
  services.parliament.uk/bills/
Childcare Act 2006 http://www.opsi.gov.uk/acts/acts2006/ukpga_20060021_en_1
Children Act 2004 http://www.opsi.gov.uk/acts/acts2004/ukpga_20040031_en_1
The Children's Legal Centre www.childrenslegalcentre.com
Child Support Agency www.csa.gov.uk/
Department of Health, National Service Framework for Children http://www.dh.gov.uk/
  en/Healthcare/Children/DH_108
Education Reform Act 1988 http://www.opsi.gov.uk/acts/acts1988/Ukpga_19880040_en_1.htm
Every Child Matters www.dfes.gov.uk/everychildmatters
Green paper 1997 Excellence for All Children: Meeting Special Educational Needs
  http://www.inclusive.co.uk/greenpap/maindoc.shtml
Health and Social Care Act 2001 http://www.opsi.gov.uk/Acts/acts2001/ukpga_
  20010015_en_1
Office of Public Sector Information http://www.opsi.gov.uk/acts
Special Educational Needs and Disability Act 2001 www.hmso.gov.uk/acts/acts2001/
  20010010.htm

Child health

Institute of Child Health and Great Ormond Street Hospital for Children Joint Website
  www.ich.ucl.ac.uk/ich/index.html
National Childbirth Trust (NCT) http://www.nct.org.uk/home
National Statistics Online, The Health of Children and Young People www.statistics.gov.
  uk/children/

Inclusion

Alliance for Inclusive Education http://www.allfie.org.uk/
Centre for Accessible Environments http://www.cae.org.uk/
Commission for Equality and Human Rights http://www.equalityhumanrights.com/
DCSF Special educational needs (SEN) and disability
  http://www.dcsf.gov.uk/everychildmatters/earlyyears/sendisability/sendisability/
National Association of SEN http://www.nasen.org.uk/
Play England http://www.playengland.org.uk/Page.asp
Social Exclusion Tax Force http://www.cabinetoffice.gov.uk/social_exclusion_task_force.aspx

Learning at university

Assessment for Learning http://www.northumbria.ac.uk/cetl_afl/
Education Subject Centre, ESCalate http://escalate.ac.uk/
MEDAL: developing students' academic literacy in CS and ECS http://medal.unn.ac.uk/
    (archived)
Write Now, student authorship project http://www.writenow.ac.uk/student_authorship.html

Multi-agency services and policy

SureStart Children's Centres http://www.dcsf.gov.uk/everychildmatters/earlyyears/
    surestart/surestartchildrenscentres/childrenscentres/
The Children's plan http://www.dcsf.gov.uk/childrensplan/ and http://www.dcsf.gov.
    uk/everychildmatters/about/childrensplan/childrensplan/
Children's Trusts http://www.dcsf.gov.uk/everychildmatters/about/aims/childrenstrusts/
    childrenstrusts/
The Children's Workforce Development Council (CWDC) http://www.cwdcouncil.org.uk/
Every Child Matters http://www.dcsf.gov.uk/everychildmatters/about/
Safeguarding and Social Care http://www.dcsf.gov.uk/everychildmatters/safeguarding
    andsocialcare/

Graduate employment and further study

Academic Jobs UK http://www.jobs.ac.uk/
CV Builder https://www.cvbuilder-advice-resources.co.uk/careersadvice/
Children and Young People Now http://www.cypnow.co.uk/.
Graduate Jobs http://www.graduate-jobs.com/gj/index.jsp
Graduate Teacher Training Registry (GTTR) http://www.gttr.ac.uk
Milkround http://milkround.com/
Postgraduate Studentships http://www.postgraduatestudentships.co.uk
Prospects http://www.prospects.ac.uk/
Target Jobs http://targetjobs.co.uk/graduate-jobs/
Teacher Training Agency (TTA) http://www.tda.gov.uk/Recruit.aspx.

Index

Please note that case studies, tables and worked examples are in *italic* print